A Feminist I:
Reflections from Academia

D1373635

A Feminist I:
Reflections from Academia

CHRISTINE OVERALL

broadview press

CANADIAN CATALOGUING IN PUBLICATION DATA

Overall, Christine, 1949–
    A feminist I: reflections from academia
Includes bibliographical references.
ISBN 1-55111-219-1

1. Feminist theory.   2. Universities and colleges – Moral and ethical aspects.
3. Knowledge, Theory of.   4. Autobiography.   I. Title.

HQ1190.003 1998   305.42'01   C98-932112-6

BROADVIEW PRESS, LTD.
is an independent, international publishing house, incorporated in 1985.

North America
Post Office Box 1243, Peterborough, Ontario, Canada K9J 7H5
3576 California Road, Orchard Park, New York, USA 14127
TEL (705) 743-8990; FAX (705) 743-8353; E-MAIL 75322.44@compuserve.com

United Kingdom and Europe
Turpin Distribution Services, Ltd., Blackhorse Rd.,
Letchworth, Hertfordshire, SG6 1HN
TEL (1462) 672555; FAX (1462) 480947; E-MAIL turpin@rsc.org

Australia
St. Clair Press, Post Office Box 287, Rozelle, NSW 2039
TEL (612) 818-1942; FAX (612) 418-1923

www.broadviewpress.com

Broadview Press gratefully acknowledges the support of the Ontario
Arts Council, and the Ministry of Canadian Heritage. We acknowledge
the financial support of the Government of Canada through the Book
Publishing Industry Development Program for our publishing activities.

Cover design by Anne Hodgets.
Typeset by Colin MacKenzie and Zack Taylor, Black Eye Design.

Printed in Canada

10 9 8 7 6 5 4 3 2 1

To the memory of my father,
Alexander Kenzie Overall

Contents

Acknowledgments

This book has come together thanks to the patience, kindness, and support of many people.

First, I am very grateful to Don LePan and Michael Harrison of Broadview Press for their enthusiasm about my manuscript and their encouragement to do it my way. Thanks also to production editor Barbara Conolly, and copy editor Betsy Struthers.

Earlier versions of some chapters appeared in print elsewhere. A version of Chapter 2, "Role Muddles," was published under the title "Role Muddles: The Stereotyping of Feminists" as No. 21 of the "Feminist Perspectives" Series, by the Canadian Research Institute for the Advancement of Women, March, 1992. I gratefully acknowledge their permission to publish a revised form of it here. I also acknowledge with gratitude the women who gave the paper from which this chapter developed an encouraging reception, in particular those who were present at the 1991 meeting of the Canadian Women's Studies Association, and the reviewers for CRIAW's Feminist Perspectives Series.

An earlier version of Chapter 5, "Nowhere at Home," was originally published with the title "'Nowhere at Home': Toward a Phenomenology of Working-Class

Consciousness," in *This Fine Place So Far From Home: Voices of Academics From the Working Class*, edited by C.L. Barney Dews and Carolyn Leste Law (Philadelphia: Temple University Press, 1995): 209-20.

An earlier version of Chapter 6, "Feeling Fraudulent," was published under the title "Feeling Fraudulent: Some Moral Quandaries of a Feminist Instructor," in *Educational Theory* 47, No. 1 (Winter, 1997): 1-13. The original copyright is held by the journal and the Board of Trustees of the University of Illinois. I am grateful for their permission to include the paper here in revised form. I also thank Donna Ede of the Queen's University Faculty Association for her prompt and thorough response to my request for bibliographic sources for this chapter, and Mark Weisberg and Susan Wilcox of the Queen's University Instructional Development Centre for the papers and books they lent me and their support of my interest in teaching. I am particularly grateful to Mark for giving me Mary Rose O'Reilly's book, *The Peaceable Classroom*, at just the point in my work on this chapter when I most needed inspiration.

I thank Shelley Tremain for her invitation to write about disability in Chapter 7, "Passing for Normal," and for her continuing encouragement even when I lacked the confidence to do so.

Finally, I am grateful to Maureen Ford, Michelle Switzer, and Jane Isaacs-Doyle for their helpful comments on earlier versions of Chapter 8, "Personal Histories, Social Identities, and Feminist Philosophical Inquiry." I also thank the audiences at the Twentieth Annual Conference of the Canadian Society for Women in Philosophy (1997), the Centenary Conference of the

Philosophy Doctoral Programme at the University of Toronto (1997), and the Queen's University Department of Philosophy Colloquium series (1997-98), for their questions and remarks in response to this chapter.

At Queen's University, I extend sincere thanks to Dean Robert Silverman and Associate Deans John Dixon, Roberta Hamilton, and Patrick O'Neill. I value their support and their lived example that doing scholarly work is not incompatible with being an academic administrator. I also thank all of the hard-working staff women in the "deanery," especially Natalie Forknall and Diane Reid.

I am grateful to my colleagues in Women's Studies at Queen's University, especially Bev Baines, Sue Hendler, Roberta Lamb, Audrey Kobayashi, Eleanor MacDonald, Terrie Easter Sheen, and Pamela Dickey Young, and my colleagues in the Department of Philosophy, especially Alistair Macleod, Stephen Leighton, Michael Fox, Christine Sypnowich, David Bakhurst, Jackie Duffin, and Carlos Prado. Special thanks to Maxine Wilson and Jackie Doherty of the Queen's Philosophy Department, who patiently and efficiently assisted me with the work entailed by this book—above and beyond the call of duty.

I want to thank, far too tardily, all my former professors in the Department of Philosophy at the University of Toronto, in particular Danny Goldstick, Hans Herzberger, John Slater, and the late David Savan. Thank you to Wayne Sumner for his ongoing encouragement. Special appreciation goes to Jack Stevenson, my PhD thesis supervisor, who has continued to advise me wisely and well for years beyond the day when he ceased to have any responsibility for my work.

I owe a great deal to the hundreds of outstanding students whom I have taught at Marianopolis College and at Queen's University. I particularly thank Harriet Simand, Peninah Brickman, Carolyn McLeod, Jason Robert, Denise Drury, Blaine Rehkopf, Sharon Read, and Jane Isaacs-Doyle for their friendship, and Jennifer Parks, Andrea Nicki, and Christine Koggel, whom I am delighted to have as colleagues in feminist philosophy.

I am grateful to Beth Morris and Winnie MacInnis, and to the Re-evaluation Counseling communities in Canada and the United States, which taught me everything I know about listening. I also thank all my friends who are part of the Kingston and Area Precision Skating Teams and the Greater Kingston Chorus of Sweet Adelines. They exemplify dedication to their art, and have kindly tolerated my absences while writing this book. Special thanks to coach Rhonda McKnight and to former "big sister" Kathy Silver.

Thank you to Adriana Vanderhelm, Jan Miller, and Diana Wyatt, whose assistance, in very different ways, has made it possible for me to continue to write.

I thank the staff at the *Kingston Whig-Standard*, especially Steve Lukits and Paul Schliessman, for giving me the experience of writing for a non-academic audience, and for extending permission in my column for me to follow my interests and my intuitions.

Finally, I lovingly thank my mother, Dorothy Overall, who is my most generous fan; my husband, Ted Worth, without whose devoted care this book could not have been written; my son, Devon Worth, whose example of self-confidence and good humour continues to inspire me; and my daughter, Narnia Worth, a challenging

philosopher and moral exemplar. All of them have tolerated my role muddles, nursed me lovingly through a
major illness, cheered me on when I took up a new job as
Associate Dean, and supported me as a writer—despite
the embarrassment my autobiographical revelations may
sometimes have caused them.

CHAPTER 1

Introduction:
A Feminist Od[d]yssey

I am a feminist. Feminism is the heart of who I am, not only as an academic, but as a citizen and an individual.

As I understand it, feminism is comprised of the well-founded belief that girls and women are legally, politically, and socially disadvantaged on the grounds of their sex; the ethical stance that this oppression is morally wrong; and the pragmatic commitment to ending injustice to all female human beings.

For me, feminism is also a scholarly and creative project, and a role whose epistemic contours and moral challenges I continue to explore. As a feminist academic I have many stories to tell about those explorations. This book is, in part, a work of feminist "theoretical autobiography" (Middleton 1993, 179). It starts from a collection of experiential stories—which is, of course, where, classically, feminist thinking begins—and chronicles some stages of my feminist od[d]yssey in the university.

I call it an od[d]yssey because I am conscious of the eccentricity of my journey through academia. On the one hand, my academic path has been entirely ordinary and unexceptional: BA, MA, and PhD degrees, followed (after a nine-year stint at a Quebec CÉGEP) by a university appointment in which I moved up through the ranks from assistant to associate and then to full professor. But on the other hand, my identities, both ascribed and chosen, as a woman and as a feminist, have made my academic situation anomalous by the standards set by and for the average white male faculty member.

"In telling their stories," write Sidonie Smith and Julia Watson, "narrators take up models of identity that are culturally available" (Smith and Watson 1996, 9, emphasis in original removed). But that cannot be the whole account, for women of my generation in academia have had to make up our professional and personal identities as we go along, dealing with the challenges and contradictions that ineluctably arise. The models were not already existing, waiting for women to try on, but had to be created, tentatively, maybe fearfully, with little or no prior observation of women in comparable situations. My academic generation was educated by men and, indeed, in my entire undergraduate education I was not taught by a single woman. Hence, our condition has been what Carolyn Heilbrun calls "liminality" (Heilbrun 1998), living on or beyond the threshold of old concepts of what women can and should do. In this necessarily ambiguous state we slip through the existing classifications of women's roles, rejecting traditional precepts about what women can and cannot, should and should not do.

There is little wonder we are sometimes disoriented. "Only certain kinds of stories become intelligible as they fit the managed framework, the imposed system" (Smith and Watson 1996, 11, emphasis in original removed). Our stories—the stories of women and also the stories of people of colour; of gays, lesbians, and bisexuals; of disabled persons; and of individuals from working class backgrounds—do not always fit an environment generated both by and for traditional academics. And when we find that our stories are unintelligible within the "imposed system," we are obliged to try to change the system, to expand the "managed framework" so that it can accommodate us. Our liminal situation provides us with both the means and the motivation to revision the conventional terms set by the university.

Like Marianna De Marco Torgovnick's *Crossing Ocean Parkway*, this series of reflections from my academic life is animated by repeated "crossing[s] between personal history and intellectual life" (Torgovnick 1994, x-xi). *A Feminist I* is intended both to exemplify and to explore the justification of the use of "confessions" and autobiography in scholarly research and teaching, particularly within the context of feminist philosophy. While this book is not primarily a memoir, it draws upon what Annette Kuhn (1995) calls "memory work." I attempt to use my own experiences, both recent and remote, to gain insights into feminism and academia. From a first-person perspective, I reflect upon the significance of socioeconomic class, gender and sex, disability, feminist research and teaching, and the politics of and demands made by the modern university. Throughout the book I am interested in exploring ethical, social, and epistemological issues generated through the intersection of identities—feminist and academic—in the context of debates about political correctness and other paradoxes of emancipatory politics within the university.

Some authors have suggested that the use of confessions in academic writing has virtually attained the status of a fad, or at least a "trend" (Miller 1997, 981, 999-1000). "Th[e] public support for confession has affected all the academic disciplines in which self-expression is given value, from sociology to literature to the visual arts" (Perillo 1997, A56). Indeed, there are many recent examples of autobiographical and confessional feminist academic writing (see Miller 1991, Kaplan 1993,[1] Greene and Kahn 1993, Torgovnick 1994,[2] Ellis 1995,[3] and Kuhn 1995[4]). One difference between their work and mine is that while theirs is located within such disciplines as literary studies, French studies, English literature, sociology, and cultural studies, mine is specifically and intentionally philosophical in nature.[5] I engage in philosophy that arises out of my situation as a woman, as a feminist, and as an academic.

In writing this book, my reflections are sustained by the conviction that, if "writing is a significant exercise of selfhood" (Quinby 1992, 306), in philosophical writing it makes a difference who you are and what your experiences are. In my scholarly work this conviction is hardwon. The kind of background and training I had as an

---

1 But see also the doubts Kaplan later expresses about the effects on her personal and professional life of writing a memoir (Kaplan 1997).

2 In light of my own concern for the significance of class differences, I find it significant that Torgovnick describes her book as, in part, a "class narrative" (1994, 10).

3 Ellis describes her book as "experimental ethnography," which she defines as "a multilayered, intertextual case study that integrates private and social experience and ties autobiographical to sociological writing" (Ellis 1995, 3).

4 See Kuhn's discussion of the significance of her working-class background to her education and her choices as an academic sociologist (pp. 84-103).

5 One recent example of the use of personal experience, the author's own and that of others, within philosophical inquiry is Brison (1997).

academic philosopher required ignoring one's own specific experiences and personal history, ignoring one's social
identities, ignoring one's changing needs and desires and
motivations. Torgovnick describes the usual process of
academic writing as "like building an armadillo: an
armored shell designed to repel criticisms that one sets
gingerly before colleagues to run for its life" (Torgovnick
1994, 70). When I was a student there was a taboo—a
taboo that is still inculcated, I find, in many of the students who come to my classes fresh from training in
humanities subjects such as English and history—against
writing in the first person. This taboo is highlighted in
Alice Kaplan's comments on her training as a theorist of
French literature:

> Personal motivation. We didn't think about personal
> motivation. We thought of ourselves in the service of
> difficulty, absence, impossibility…. Curiosity about too
> many things was discouraged; author's lives, for
> example, were beneath us. (Kaplan 1993, 173)

In this book I break the taboo of my philosophical training by deliberately and explicitly using my own academic life experience as the primary resource for my philosophizing.

My earliest inclination to use my own life as a
resource for philosophy arose out of my experiences as a
mother, which inspired an early paper in which I
appealed to my lived relationship to my children as the
basis for critiquing the notorious philosophical "problem
of other minds" (Overall 1988). Then, after years of writing impersonal philosophy, including a great deal of
impersonal feminist philosophy (e.g., Overall 1987a,

1993), I began to experience an impulse to give the subtitle "confessions" to virtually every "scholarly" work I wrote. This feeling was fostered, in part, by my work as the writer of a weekly feminist column for my city's local paper.[6] While my background and training in analytic philosophy had always required that I write clearly and directly, the need and desire to reach through my column a diverse, non-academic, public audience, to be accessible, to be lively and interesting, and to move people, transformed my goals as a writer.

Yet the necessity of communicating with different audiences is not a new feature of my life. For a girl from a working class background, the first of her family ever to attend university, finding the right words to reach particular audiences very early became an urgent necessity. I had to find a way to be understood by, if not acceptable to, people from very different class origins than mine, and I had to do so in a way that would not compromise the values in terms of which I define my feminism.

Some feminists describe this relationship to the audience as a result of the "drive to connect" (Frey 1993, 44). But, as a feminist philosopher, my motivation has been not so much to connect with my audience as simply to get its attention. In writing and speaking about philosophy I am acting upon my urge to interpret human culture and to figure out difficult issues *in public*, that is, with the reading or listening audience's acknowledgement. As a feminist, I have often faced sceptical audiences, whose initial response to my presentations placed the onus on me to show why they should find my views worth noticing, let alone plausible. In making myself heard by these

---

6 The column is entitled "In Other Words" and appears on Mondays in the Kingston *Whig-Standard*.

various audiences, my aim has always been to initiate reception without expecting agreement. One way to encourage the audience to listen to me is to appeal to stories from my own experiences. So, finding methods of speaking to different groups required discovering ways to be public about what is personal. I had to become approachable. In employing the genre of theoretical autobiography, I am motivated both by the fearful desire to reveal who I am, and by the conviction that appealing to personal experience will disarm audiences and provide an opening for my political values.

> For the marginalized woman, autobiographical language may serve as a coinage that purchases entry into the social and discursive economy.... Deploying autobiographical practices that go against the grain, she may constitute an 'I' that becomes a place of creative and, by implication, political intervention. (Watson and Smith 1992, xix)

Early versions of several of the chapters in this book were originally presented to a variety of different audiences, ranging from a large group of primary and secondary school teachers and teachers in training (Chapter 3) and audiences comprised of women's studies scholars and graduate students (Chapters 2 and 5), to an audience of administrators and academics interested in pedagogy (Chapter 4) and an audience of mostly mainstream, analytically-trained philosophers (Chapter 8).

I'm inclined to say that its original audience helped to influence the character of each of the chapters. Yet to state that relationship in such a way implies a writer and speaker who is too passive. Rather, it is always *my view* of the audience—my understanding of its collective personality; its hidden needs, wants, and agenda; and its political presuppositions—that shapes the issues as I advance them and the arguments that I use. By choosing how to present my experiences and by making aspects of myself available to my audiences, I also become an active participant in the development of the feminist I that the audience hears. As a writer and speaker I try to influence and persuade my audience and my readers, even as I am remaking myself. To "exercise selfhood" through writing is also to recreate the self. As Crispin Sartwell puts it,

> All my writing, and I think this is true of a lot of people, has been aimed primarily at treating myself; I am always telling myself what I think I need to hear, am always writing the books I think I need to read. My books are attempts to reconfigure my self or to manufacture a new self. (Sartwell 1998, 13)[7]

While I do not assume that others necessarily have the same experiences as mine, I hope that listeners and readers, both inside and outside the academy—and especially those who are feminists, regardless of whether they share my history and my version of feminism—will experience a resonance with my stories.

Although we tend to have an acute sense of our specificity, as if our experience, like a thumbprint, were

---

7 Jane Gallop suggests, "we have to think constructed somehow other than in opposition to authentic" (Gallop 1995, 15). The constructed self (the only kind there is) can also be an authentic self, that is, a persona whom I have consciously chosen, and who espouses the ideals I value.

unique (which, of course, in a bodily sense it is),
autobiography theory has usefully shown that this
uniqueness is what, paradoxically, is at one and the
same time shareable and shared—and alternately
refused: not like me at all. (Miller 1997, 999)

These reflections will therefore make no great claims to
generalizability, although I have endeavoured to identify
and clarify what I believe are epistemological and moral
issues common to many feminists in academia. I share
with Carolyn Ellis the hope that "What I ha[ve] learned
from my own struggles for meaning [is] unique enough
to be interesting, yet typical enough to help others
understand important aspects of their lives" (Ellis 1995,
308).

Exploring the strengths and liabilities of our conflicting roles as feminist and academic has potential epistemic value, offering insights into such matters as how
the university works, how oppression operates, and what
paths we might take toward liberation. Though by no
means a handbook or a practical guide, *A Feminist I* is,
nonetheless, a pragmatic record of my struggles as a
feminist and what I have learned from them.

Slowly and with difficulty over the last decade and
a half, I have come to understand something about
the political and moral meanings of being a feminist,
about men and masculinism in the university, about the
demands of teaching and the needs of different groups
of students, about the effects of socio-economic class
background, and about the cultural interpretation of
disability. My understanding of these matters has come
about partly because the academic environment has forced
me to rethink my preconceptions and my behaviour.

Much of what I now believe about teaching and learning, as well as my views about feminist politics, masculinist power, and the hierarchical operations of institutions of higher learning, originated in my immersion in the realities of university life.

My understanding has also come about partly through my direct encounters with others' sometimes-unthinking reactions to my identities, both ascribed and chosen. Although these reactions were often painful to experience, I am no mere victim and do not perceive myself as one. I recognize and acknowledge the extraordinary rights and privileges I enjoy as a middle-class professional: freedom to say and write what I believe, exposure to new ideas and discoveries, professional autonomy, a good income. But inevitably, my personal confrontations with stereotypes, limitations, and injustices have had an especially powerful effect on my world view. As a person from a working-class background I needed years of bumping up against the university's covert classism before I finally learned that class background matters. And through my experience of temporary disablement, I journeyed from a place of ignorance about disability to a world in which social attitudes toward disabled persons were only too evident. In recounting what I learned through these experiences, my aim is not to claim the status of the oppressed, but rather to contribute to a growing feminist understanding of oppression.

My analysis of how to respond to disagreement and conflict is greatly influenced by my experiences in Re-evaluation Counseling ("RC") (Jackins 1973, 1978a, 1978b, 1981, 1983, 1985, 1987, 1989, 1992). RC is a form of peer counselling, which emphasizes mutual help and the exchange of listening time to enable participants to emerge from past distresses and free themselves from oppressive social patterns. From RC I have learned to respect though not always believe people's expressions of emotion, to emphasize shared opportunities for listening and speaking, and to go beyond hopelessness to a vision of social change that permits all human beings to flourish.

In reaching out to various audiences, therefore, I tend to interpret my function as being that of a feminist intellectual "Ms Fix-It," who tries to move past the litanizing of feminist complaints to providing proposals for change. As a result, several chapters close with my suggestions for liberating ourselves and the academic world from some of the practices and ideologies that hold sexism and other oppressive ideologies in place. Like Naomi Scheman, I believe that

> it's just not true that the real world starts where the campus ends; ... I think that [students'] lives are real lives, and making a difference to them is making a difference in the real world; ... what we do together can be radically transformative, not only of [students] but of the other lives [they] touch. (Scheman 1995, 109)

In each of the chapters that follow I explore a different story, an aspect of my experience as a feminist academic and the conclusions that I draw from it. While some chapters are more theoretical than others, all are intended to exemplify my practice of reflecting on the meaning of my situation in academia. In Chapter 2, I begin by describing some examples of feminist political and moral "role muddles," generated by the conflicting expectations that arise from roles that are socially dissonant. I am interested in how feminists are policed, both by those who fear or despise feminism and by those who expect feminism to be a panacea. Sometimes feminists also police each other, and the result is not solidarity but rather ethical confusion about what feminism is and what feminists should do. Situating feminist role muddles within the context of the media focus on "political correctness" and its effects on feminism, I connect them with ongoing debates about academic freedom and free speech, especially within teaching. Feminist role muddles have something important to tell us about what feminism is.

This exploration is followed, in Chapter 3, by reflections on feminists' often-ambiguous relationship with men in academia. "Women and Men in Education" discusses general political features of the situation of women and men, whether as students, staff, or faculty; the culture of sexism within the universities; and possible methods by which gender oppression and internalized oppression might be diminished. I try to show how feminist insights about oppression and internalized oppression, forms of communication, and the unrecognized values of emotion, can be given direct application within university committees and classrooms.

Role muddles may also originate from the varied and even conflicting demands made by different academic classes. The experience of teaching each year a new but forever-young student cohort gives the illusion that teaching itself is always the same. Yet the attempt to prepare and educate students must necessarily be flexible, to adjust to the varying needs, backgrounds, and goals of the always-unique individuals whom we instruct. In Chapter 4, "A Tale of Two Classes," I describe two different groups of students who took my favourite course, "Philosophy and Feminism," and the ways in which their various motives, assumptions, and beliefs forced me to reshape my pedagogical assumptions and my approaches to teaching. The disorientation that I experienced when I realized that the second class could not be treated in the way I treated the first posed a profound challenge to my moral and political commitments as a feminist.

There is, of course, another meaning of "class" that should be just as immediate and important for classroom instructors. Starting from recollections of my working-class background, Chapter 5, "Nowhere At Home," develops what I call the phenomenology of a working-class academic's consciousness. As a tenured academic I now belong to the middle class, but I grew up in a working-class household and neighbourhood. To have a working-class background is to possess a feature that simultaneously makes it more difficult to acclimatize to the academic environment and also offers potential insights into the class-based operations of the university. In Chapter 5 I focus upon the discontinuities—in culture, expectations, values, priorities, and background knowledge—generated by the class mobility that higher education produces, and what I have learned from them.

The experience of being transposed from working-class family to middle-class academic engenders, for me, the feeling of being an imposter. Chapter 6, "Feeling Fraudulent," examines the feeling of academic fraudulence, and the connection of this feeling to moral quandaries in the situation of university instructors, especially those who are feminists. The feeling of being a fraud who has, through accident or deception, infiltrated the ivory tower, is, I suggest, a not-surprising manifestation of the feminist academic identity. If I believe that I have not mastered the conflicting demands of my roles, then I am likely to feel like an imposter. When, in addition, I am at a life stage when my students are likely to regard me as a mother rather than as a generational peer, the combination of ageism with sexism exacerbates feelings of insecurity and role anomie. Rather than viewing it only negatively, I try to discern the implicit resources that feeling fraudulent may offer and use it to attempt a resolution or at least a revisioning of some ethical problems in university teaching.

In Chapter 7, "Passing for Normal," I draw upon my experiences of temporary disablement and my encounters with ableism, a phenomenon exacerbated by its connections with ageism. In their response to persons with disability many university faculty reveal a deep discontinuity between their moral ideals and gritty academic reality. My experience of being profoundly disabled while being pressured to pass as non-disabled, of being a medical patient while being expected to continue to be an "able-bodied" academic, generated role muddles that threatened my loyalty to the university. The requirement to deny, downplay, or protect others from one's identities (whether of class, sexual orientation, or ability) encourages persons who do not fit the "managed framework" of academia to attempt to adapt and assimilate or to disappear altogether.

All of these chapters are deliberately personal and experiential in method and tone. Yet the personal is never straightforwardly self-evident and unadorned or unrehearsed. As Gallop wryly remarks, "when the personal appears [in educational contexts] it is always as the

result of a process of im-personation [*sic*], a process of
performing the personal for a public" (Gallop 1995, 9).
Despite my appeals to personal experiences and social
identities throughout these chapters, I am aware of the
potential drawbacks of using personal experience within
philosophical inquiry (Perillo 1997, A56).

> It's important to remember and record. To set the
> record straight, to get the story out. But we cannot
> afford to make memorializing a fetish: the sign of desire
> once wounded and forever enshrined. (Miller 1997,
> 1013)

However, as I assume throughout this book, the dangers of an uncritical, too-respectful appeal to experience
do not mean that experience should not be used at all,
only that it must be used critically and with care: "For it
is through manipulation that one gains power over an
experience in which one originally was powerless—that,
at least, is the therapeutic lesson" (Perillo 1997, A56).
Thus, this book is intended both as a demonstration and
as an evaluation of the use of experience in academic
writing.

> [E]xperience is not infrequently played as the trump
> card of authenticity, the last word of personal truth,
> forestalling all further discussion, let alone analysis.
> Nevertheless, experience is undeniably a key category of
> everyday knowledge, structuring people's lives in
> important ways. So, just as I know perfectly well that
> the whole idea is a fiction and a lure, part of me also
> 'knows' that my experience—my memories, my feelings
> —are important because these things make me what I

am, make me different from everyone else. Must they be consigned to a compartment separate from the part of me that thinks and analyses? Can the idea of experience not be taken on board—if with a degree of caution—by cultural theory, rather than being simply evaded or, worse, consigned to the domain of sentimentality and nostalgia? (Kuhn 1995, 28)

I place the most theoretical component of this book— Chapter 8, "Personal Histories, Social Identities, and Feminist Philosophical Inquiry"—at the end because it evaluates the general justification of the methods used throughout the earlier chapters. After exploring the arguments for and against the use of and appeal to individual histories and social identities within feminist education and research, this chapter concludes by presenting my rationale for relying in so much of my work upon appeals to experience.

As I finish this book I have recently assumed a new academic identity. In my new capacity as a university administrator, I am immersed in handling the role muddles generated through the assumption of formidable amounts of responsibility together with the deployment of limited forms of academic power—while also trying to maintain my political commitments and moral integrity. As an academic feminist who is at once engaged with political struggles in the university and committed to scholarly reflection about the meanings of those struggles and their ethical ambiguities, I know that my feminist od[d]yssey is not finished.

CHAPTER 2

Role Muddles

> As feminist writers we know we cannot speak for
> anyone else: vain, unethical venture. Nor can we ignore
> or disregard the consequences of our writing. (Livia
> 1989, 33)

Several years ago I wrote a fairly conventional feminist
theoretical paper on the dangers and liabilities of setting
up isolated individual women as role models in institutions where they almost inevitably experience serious role
conflicts and constraints (Overall 1987b). This chapter,
however, is not about role models but rather role *muddles*,
and, unlike my earlier effort, it must and will be written
primarily in the first person, rather than in the apparently neutral and theoretical third person.

My identities, combined, create what I call role
muddles—a set of discontinuities, contradictions, and
ambiguities generated by conflicting expectations arising
from socially incompatible roles. In the role muddle
experience there is simultaneously both confusion about
what I should be or do, as a feminist, and resistance to
the individual and social voices that seem only too willing and eager to tell me what I should be and do, as a
feminist. While I experience role muddles as a feminist
mother, friend, and partner, I shall primarily focus here
on my role muddles as a feminist academic: that is, as a
teacher in the classroom, as a scholar of feminist philosophy, and as a privileged feminist among women more
disadvantaged than I.

Role muddles arise as I attempt to deal with both teaching about feminism and teaching as a feminist, as I do feminist research, and as I encounter feminist political issues on campus. I am compelled to juggle competing demands, expectations, and role requirements generated within the university. My suspicion is that most feminist academics encounter role muddles because of the discontinuities between the history and agenda of the universities within which we work and our own personal politics. Our interpretations of what feminist politics requires and demands of us vary, and many of us are in the process of figuring out what behaviour is morally compatible with our feminist commitments.

I shall begin by describing examples of my role muddles, examples which range from the fairly personal to the more overtly political. My conviction is that these examples share some Wittgensteinian "family resemblances," although they appear fairly diverse. For the social process of defining and constructing feminism and feminists has led to the stereotyping of what a feminist is—a stereotyping created partly by some feminists and partly by some who are not feminists.

1) I get a call from a woman in a nearby city. She is phoning to invite me to present a workshop at an upcoming non-academic conference just four weeks away. Careful questioning reveals that there is no pay for this work; that her group cannot afford to accommodate me overnight, so that I must go and return in one day; that they prefer that I take the bus rather than the train or plane because the bus is cheaper; and that the presentation must be at the elementary level for an audience with no prior knowledge of the topic.

This is work I have done many times before. My schedule is already jammed with responsibilities: student essays to grade, classes to prepare, papers to write, presentations to give, committee meetings to attend, my children's activities to supervise. In the end, I turn down the invitation, but not without facing considerable disappointment and even reproach from my caller who suggests that, as a feminist, I should be willing and even eager to do this work. I feel guilty and confused.

My first role muddle, then, arises in response to what appears to be the expectation that as a feminist academic I will always be available and accessible to other individuals and organizations; that I will give without stinting to every current political project; that I will donate my time and energy for feminist conferences, committees, demonstrations, publications, workshops, and lecture series that want my labour; and that I will always be delighted to offer a willing ear and sympathetic shoulder for distressed persons of both sexes.

A central criterion for evaluating me as a good colleague and teacher is whether I successfully sustain an "open door policy." Significantly, no other profession—doctor, physiotherapist, psychiatrist, social worker, lawyer—that I can think of demands this unconstrained access. Significantly, the nearest similarity is to the role of mother and to other gender-stereotyped work such as waitressing and secretarial services. For these functions, it is believed to be acceptable to interrupt the individuals who fulfil them because the work is not considered valuable, independent, or autonomous.

Do I sound like a curmudgeon as I describe these situations? My impression is that these role expectations, and the feelings that arise in response to them, exist not just because I am a woman and a mother—and women and mothers in particular are expected to be predictably self-sacrificing and beneficent—but because, more specifically, I am a feminist, and feminists are expected, as part of our political duty, to offer these benefits. To be a feminist is to be committed to both service to and accessibility for other persons and programs. Of course, given the condition the world is in, what I do is never enough and is never regarded as being enough, yet more is always expected of me than of the man down the hall precisely because I am a feminist. Hence the questions that prompt this role muddle are: how much should I do as a feminist? and when can I justifiably say no?

2) My second role muddle arises in connection with the public manifestations of my work as a feminist academic. It comes up, for example, when in discussions or reviews[1] of my published work, a critic argues that as a feminist I should not have made a certain argument or included a certain paper in an anthology I've edited, or even that my views suggest that I am not really a feminist after all. The pain I experience on hearing or reading such claims is quite different from my reaction to being discussed or reviewed by non-feminist writers who are much less likely to assail me on grounds of alleged feminist inconsistency or disloyalty. The fear of rejection, the wish to be supported and liked (or at least not attacked), the concern to be politically correct and consistent, the defensiveness, and the anxiety about risk-taking are far greater when my audience is feminists. Perhaps

---

1 Cf. Tancred-Sheriff (1990, 1) on the corresponding constraints (self-)imposed by being a feminist reviewer.

unreasonably, I find myself wanting to be recognized for who I am as a feminist academic and also to be accepted and nurtured by the people whom I think of as my special peers and colleagues.

This role muddle arises not only when I am performing feminism, myself, but also when I witness others performing feminism. When a feminist addresses an audience of non-feminists, I feel a special anxiety for her: I fear for her safety, and I want her to do well. When a woman who is not a feminist expounds upon feminism in a derogatory way, I feel a special anger at her. When men who are pro-feminist discuss feminism, I feel a complicated set of mixed loyalties—part approval for their efforts, part possessiveness for the integrity of feminism as a women's movement. When anyone—feminist or not—criticises a woman publicly, I feel a pull to defend her, sometimes even in spite of the unprogressive views the woman may have, and the deservedness of the criticism. When women gossip about other women, and especially when I gossip about other women and other feminists, I feel a particular sense of guilt and self-compromise. On the one hand, I don't want women to be criticised, yet sometimes it seems women should be criticised, deserve to be criticised. In these cases, then, my role muddles stem from my uncertainty about appropriate behaviour toward other women in public: unconditional support or conditional support (but conditional on what?), and from my suspicion that, whether I like it or not, what other women do in public, and what others, of either sex, say about feminism, will reflect upon me.

So my role muddle here is twofold: have I indeed adopted views and behaviours that are inconsistent with feminism? and, what, if anything, do I owe my female and/or feminist peers when I respond to and evaluate their work?

3) Role muddles also arise in the women's studies classroom, and students are troubled by them. Women's studies students at Queen's University, for example, sometimes wonder what beliefs, attitudes, and behaviour are appropriate for them as feminists, and what is the right response to feminists whose behaviour they disapprove of. For example, Sharilyn MacGregor, a Queen's student, wrote the following in the Queen's student paper (1990, 10):

> I have seen clear ideological divisions arise in Women's Studies classes.... The splitting is often antagonistic and manifests itself in an unspoken hierarchy of 'political correctness.'... For instance, those who believe that change is possible without revolution and separatism are made to feel as if they have been 'co-opted' by patriarchy; or they are called liberal (the dreaded 'l' word). On the other hand, those who embrace radical feminism are accused of being self-righteous, self-appointed gatekeepers of the entire movement.

Many of my feminist students—a hardy, hard-working, dedicated bunch who struggle to stay alive on a conservative, sometimes repressive campus—want to know what a real feminist is and does—that is, what the political bottom line is for feminism, and whom they can trust.

As a feminist professor I suspect I may have some responsibility to respond to my students' role muddles in the classroom—but that is difficult when I'm still struggling with my own pedagogical role muddles which develop in response to my feminist students' often conflicting expectations. Kathryn Morgan (1987) has described some of the paradoxes generated by our diverse responsibilities as feminist teachers. In my experience, the most problematic are those of nurturing classroom democracy from my position of (relative) power as a tenured professor and sustaining demanding scholarly standards whilst fostering a caring environment within the class. Does a good feminist teacher impose late penalties, set final examinations, require attendance at most classes? Should I be more lenient about academic rules and regulations with my feminist students, as some of them expect, especially in view of the political work many are engaged in? How much informal counselling and hand-holding should I do? (The need is almost endless.) Should a feminist teacher be a friend to her feminist students, as Leslie Thielen-Wilson (1988) has suggested?

4) These role muddles about my position as a feminist teacher are exacerbated by my complicated and touchy relationship with my institution. As Evelyn Fox Keller and Helen Moglen (1987, 26) have observed, whereas my feminist students may expect confident and supportive mentors, many women faculty themselves

> do not actually experience themselves as powerful. Over the years they have internalized the patronizing judgments made by scornful male teachers and colleagues. Thus, even when they achieve positions of authority, they continue to feel the oppression of past struggles and the ongoing burdens of tokenism. How

can they effectively assert power if they actually feel impotent?

I suggest that the impotence that Keller and Moglen refer to is not just a feeling. There is much evidence—ranging from the dangers of sexual assault and harassment and the contempt for feminist scholarship, to women's higher workload in student counselling and committees and the paucity of women who are full professors (APA Committee on the Status of Women 1995) or hold significant administrative positions—which suggests that even tenured women in academia are relatively less powerful than their male colleagues. Not acknowledging, or perhaps not fully recognizing, these factors, students sometimes reject faculty women's perceptions of themselves and attribute to faculty women an invulnerability that they don't have (Keller and Moglen 1987, 28). In view of these diverse perceptions, then, it is difficult for me to know who I am: the strong and successful female mentor or the vulnerable and oppressed minority group member in a male-dominated institution.

As a white middle-class feminist academic, I am also aware of the institutional dangers of co-optation. The lure of a secure job with a good income invites me to buy uncritically into the traditional values of the university, to become complacent about problems of injustice outside academia, or to be over-confident about the degree to which the institution is able to separate itself from prevailing social conditions of racism, sexism, classism, and heterosexism. While the university is no ivory tower, especially for poorly-paid staff and for kids without race or class privileges, it is a relatively sheltered environment for those like me who are permitted a permanent connection via tenure.

An even more insidious form of co-optation is identified by Marilyn Frye. She points out that the presence of feminist teachers actually helps repressive systems to run better; we appear to confirm that the institution is beneficent and fair. Frye writes (1992, 31): "The better I am at teaching [a feminist perception of the world], the more truth I find and communicate, the more good I do the institution. The fact that it allows someone to stand in it and say those things gives it credit in the eyes of the students and the wider public...."

In addition, while much recent feminist writing has been critical of many feminists' complacency with respect to race, sexual orientation, class, and ethnic privilege, sometimes these criticisms seem to result in a sort of competition over how oppressed we are (Ross 1987, 212-214). Does my working-class upbringing compensate for the privileges I enjoy as a white woman? Of course not— but I still experience role muddles over the problem of how and to what extent I can and should disaffiliate, to use Frye's term (1983, 126-127), from all the various forms of my privilege. My role muddles in these instances are concerned with questions about whether and how, with all of my privileges, I can still be a genuine, and genuinely moral, feminist academic.

An Epistemological Paradox in Feminism

It might be suggested that my role muddles arise largely from the fact that there are many versions of feminism (Alcoff 1988, Delmar 1986, Offen 1988, Snitow 1990), so that a self-identified feminist may feel discomfort in confrontations with its different public manifestations.

(Indeed, the earlier quotation from Sharilyn MacGregor suggests that this is the explanation for some women's studies students' role muddles.) Nevertheless, I believe that my role muddles are not just a puzzle about what kind of feminist to call myself. Beyond the very simple explanation one might give to non-feminists and interested potential feminists, it's not clear how useful or accurate definitions of different forms of feminism might be, and I shall not attempt here to delineate the different degrees and kinds of political engagement that different forms of feminism might arguably require.

But although my role muddles are not just a matter of the definition of various versions of feminism, they do have something to do with wondering what it takes to be a feminist, what it means to be a feminist, and what is expected from a feminist. I believe other feminist academics sometimes share these questions. As Karen Offen asks, "When is a feminist really an antifeminist? What must the fundamental criteria be? And, most important politically, *who* will decide?" (1988, 129, her emphasis).

This concern for knowing what it means to be a feminist is, of course, not only an epistemological puzzle, but an ethical challenge. It comes from the real moral impulse to do the right thing, as feminists. Often when stress, overwork, fatigue, and role conflict are at their highest, the impulse to do the right thing seems to be the one remaining motive that inspires my feminist academic colleagues. Feminist theory, ethics, and practice set high moral standards for those who call themselves feminists. As Maria Lugones and Elizabeth Spelman (1987, 234) point out, "One of the ways to explore the meaning of any version of feminism is to ask what it says or implies about how people ought to treat one another." My role muddles are confusions about what could be called "feminist responsibility": what are my responsibilities, as a feminist academic, especially for and to other women, whether feminist or non-feminist? How do they fit, or fail to fit, with what others (both feminists and non-feminists) take my responsibilities to be?

During the course of the last few years I have witnessed many debates among feminists about feminist responsibilities. Among them are the following: is it consistent and justifiable for a feminist to be independently wealthy? in the military? married? wear spike heels and heavy make-up? read and enjoy Harlequin romances (Miles 1991, 93-96)? gossip about other feminists? pursue professional ambitions? aspire to institutional power? eat meat? campaign against abortion? favour the new reproductive technologies? oppose all forms of censorship? be unwilling to work collectively? downplay the importance of lesbian studies? publicly criticize the women's studies program? openly mock certain feminist theorists? While I myself do not necessarily find all of these behaviours problematic, I suggest that the moral questions they provoke are genuine and ought not to be considered either unproblematic or unanswerable.

In view of the existence of these and comparable issues, is it preferable to be lenient and permissive or strict and meticulous in delineating the feminist role and what it means to be a feminist? *Prima facie*, a wide latitude about the constitution of feminism seems appropriate, for as a feminist I am committed to valuing every woman's experience and genuinely listening to her views. Without such tolerance there is a danger of ignorance, in-fighting, and lack of solidarity with diverse forms of political expression. Perhaps I should even adopt a kind of anarchist/deconstructionist perspective on the political and moral concept of "the feminist": by refusing to define what a feminist is, by refusing to recognize or demarcate any feminist role, I reject the reification of that which is, after all, a cultural artefact, a social identity that is fluid, changing, and open to constant reappraisal and reconstruction.

But how far can such tolerance go? We know now that no experience is an unanalyzable given, and that some forms of experience may conceal rather than reveal political repression and exploitation. So the credulous endorsement of everyone's experience and views, under the rubric of a receptive feminism, could permit tolerance of the conservative status quo and even encourage the flourishing of reactionary attacks upon the few political advances we have made. An uncritical moral relativism on the part of feminists could unwittingly validate an anti-progressive, anti-feminist moral anarchy.

In thinking about this question of lenience or strictness with respect to delineating feminism, I have been assisted by Ann Snitow's discussion of a comparable split in feminists' understanding of "woman." As Snitow (1990, 9) puts it,

> a common divide keeps forming in both feminist thought and action between the need to build the identity 'woman' and give it solid political meaning and the need to tear down the very category woman and dismantle its all too solid history…. [F]eminists—and indeed most women—live in a complex relationship to this central feminist divide. From moment to moment, we perform subtle psychological and social negotiations about just how gendered we choose to be.

I suggest that in the role muddles some of us experience as academic feminists, a familiar debate about the meaning of the pronoun "we" is recreated. As the quotation from Snitow suggests, the debate originated with respect to our identity and identification as women, where the assertion that "we" are all women (a homogeneous and ahistorical category) stands in apparent opposition to the recognition that "we" are actually very different in terms of such variables as race, class, age, and sexual orientation. What Snitow (1990, 9) calls this "tension—between needing to act as women and needing an identity not overdetermined by our gender" has a political *doppelgänger* in feminists' theoretical and practical construal of our political identity: there is a significant tension between needing to be and to act as a feminist and needing an identity not over-determined by social definitions—even our own—of "the feminist." There is a tension between the need for political identity and unity as feminists and the need not to be confined or excluded by that identity and unity. In our identity and identification as feminists, the assertion that "we" are all feminists (also a homogeneous and ahistorical category) stands in apparent opposition to the recognition that "we" are actually very different, as feminists, with diverse values and political agendas.

Snitow convincingly argues that we may just have to live with—rather than resolving or reconciling—the ongoing tension between reclaiming our identity as women and dismantling our identity as women. Similarly, I suggest, because there are good reasons both for opposing a relativist view of the moral limits of feminism and for tolerating wide divergence among self-confessed feminists, feminists may have to live with, and ruefully, perhaps, acknowledge, the ongoing tension between forging a strong identity as feminists and refusing to be confined by our identity as feminists. In other words, there is no neat and definitive answer to the question of how we know what a real feminist is; the very nature of feminism as a moral and political project generates an irresolvable—yet also fruitful—epistemological uncertainty about who we are and what we should do.

Political Correctness and Incorrectness

Nevertheless, the matter cannot rest with this paradoxical evenhandedness, for it is necessary to take account of the political dimensions of feminist role muddles. On the one hand, feminist academics need each other as political and personal allies, and anxiety about others' deviance from prescribed feminist norms may be, in part, an understandable fear of isolation, abandonment, and disempowerment. Yet at the same time feminist academics are expected and perhaps even forced to engage in certain forms of competition with each other over scarce resources such as jobs, salaries, promotions, grants, contracts, and publication opportunities (Keller and Moglen 1987). Proving ourselves sufficiently to be permitted to stay in the academy means that only so-called excellence is good enough—where "excellence" is defined using terms in which we have little or no say.

In an environment where women—and especially "uppity" women—are still seen as anachronisms, the handful of feminists on campus may be thought to have numbers and power out of all proportion to reality. Our feminist role muddles are, therefore, in part the artificial and awkward consequence of the tremendous visibility of women in the male-defined academic context where as somewhat privileged tokens, what other women, and especially other feminists, do is taken to reflect on me, and what I do is taken to reflect on them. The marginalizing stereotypes of feminists suggest, as Keller and Moglen put it (1987, 29), that "one resident feminist is enough for any department, ... all feminists are similar and therefore roughly interchangeable." The external stereotyping falsely labels us as "all of a kind," while seizing upon any dissent among us either as signs of weakness and inconclusiveness or as evidence of repressiveness. This is the context in which one woman (presumably by virtue of her genitalia alone) is assumed to represent "the woman's view," and in which non-feminist colleagues send students to "the" feminists[2] instead of learning about feminism themselves. Thus academic women, feminists especially, are seen not as individuals but as members of a gender class or a political monolith.

Under these conditions of desperation for allies, enforced competition, and undue visibility as tokens, it is hardly surprising that feminist academics sometimes internalize the invalidation we receive and express "horizontal hostility" toward each other,[3] in the form of an overt or covert concern for "political correctness." The concern for political correctness is a prime motivator of feminist role muddles.

But in my experience, the notion of political correctness gets used in more than one way. On some occasions,

2   A point made by Susan Boyd in a presentation at Queen's University, January 26, 1990.

3   I discuss "horizontal hostility" and internalized oppression at greater length in Chapter 3.

for example, I've been accused by other feminists of being politically incorrect in my thinking, writing, or political behaviour. But I've also been accused, by a woman who complained of feeling afraid of people like me, of *using* the charge of political incorrectness myself, to squelch genuine and important views and in particular to curtail "compassion and justice for men" (Friedman 1990, 26).

These experiences reflect an insidious sequence of political developments. First, the ideas of political correctness and incorrectness are used—perhaps not always intentionally, but nevertheless often with painful results—to monitor feminist attitudes, beliefs, and behaviour. Then, individuals and institutions on the right plaintively complain of the supposed "tyranny" of progressive movements such as feminism which allegedly use the concepts of politically correct and incorrect to stifle free speech and censor innovation. For example,

> '[P]olitically correct' has become a sarcastic jibe used by conservatives and classical liberals alike to describe what they see as a growing intolerance, a closing of debate, a pressure to conform to a radical program or risk being accused of a commonly reiterated trio of thought crimes: sexism, racism and homophobia (Bernstein 1990, 2).

An article in *Maclean's* adds, "those who oppose the forces of political correctness say that they fear the new reformers will stifle democratic processes—and bury a rich cultural tradition in the name of equality" (Fennell 1991, 43).

Of course, as Rosalie Abella points out, "[t]here is nothing wrong with being politically correct if in being

46

politically wrong we are being unfair" (Abella 1991, 17). But what is falsely implied by many critics of feminism is that some single notion of political correctness rigidly prescribes the entire feminist agenda, and that by contrast, established institutions, governments, and political movements do not themselves use notions of political correctness to regulate what is taught, broadcast, and published.

Thus, the notion of political correctness can work against feminists in two different and powerful ways: first, through the operation of internalized oppression that can impair innovation through fear of political incorrectness and, secondly, through the co-optation of the concept by those who are hostile to progressive movements such as feminism. For the most part, it is not women's interests that are served by concepts of political correctness. Instead, it is in the interests of conservative institutions to foster escalating charges of political incorrectness among the progressive elements in their midst and to encourage invidious divisions among feminists committed to radical social change.

As an undergraduate at a Canadian university during the late 1960s, I was enrolled in a third-year psychology course called "Thinking and Reasoning." The course included about eighteen students, of whom perhaps one-third were women. The professor was male. He made no secret of his view that women do not think the way men do, and it was clear that he saw this alleged difference as a flaw in women. Ironically, the women in that class on thinking and reasoning were being taught by a man who did not believe in our ability to think and reason. He often said, as if stating an incontestable matter of fact, "women are irrational" and "women let their emotions get in the way of their thinking," and many of the male students agreed with him.

Whenever he said these things, the women in the group would look at each other uncomfortably. We would roll our eyes in disgust, and once, I remember, a couple of us even went so far as to hiss after the professor made one of his pronouncements. But we never verbally objected to or argued against his views on women's abilities, and we certainly made no effort to complain about this man's sexist teaching.

I tell this story because I want to emphasize that that professor was expressing the political orthodoxy of that time. That is, he was stating the politically correct view about women's intellectual abilities, a view that dominated the universities in the 1960s. But his view was not seen as a mere expression of opinion, however orthodox; it was not seen as merely the politically correct dogmatism of the time. Instead, it was regarded as just "the way things are," the way people are. It was a straightforward expression of (unrecognized) essentialism: the view that women and men have an essential nature by virtue of their sex, without which they would not be real women or real men.[4] While the women in the class felt uncomfortable about the irony of being enrolled in a course whose conceptual foundations seemed to assume our inability to understand the material, we did not yet have the understanding of sexism that would have enabled us to challenge it. The very successful policing of thought at that time meant that no one yet understood that this man was silencing the women in his class.

---

4 According to essentialism, then, the differences between women and men cannot be merely contingent, the product of enculturation.

The point I am making here is that standards of political correctness in North America, often so entrenched as to go unnoticed, have customarily favoured the conservative status quo, or traditional political orthodoxy, not social reform. These standards of political correctness did not and do not get recognized as value judgments or political claims—until they are challenged by minorities who no longer accept the premises of inequality on which they are founded.

Accusing progressive individuals and groups of an inappropriate commitment to political correctness is, in an insidious and underhanded way, a very clever means for the upholders of the establishment to defend themselves by reversing both the responsibility and the focus of attention. It enables them to look like the champions of free speech, without requiring them to engage in actual debates about the justification of their own views. They seem to be saying that it is worse to accuse someone of sexism than to be a sexist. In other words, the current controversy over political correctness is a cover that has been developed to defend inequality by excluding or delegitimating criticisms of its moral basis.

This controversy places the focus of attention, not on the harms caused by sexism, homophobia, and racism, but rather on defending men, or heterosexuals, or whites, who, it is now alleged, are being harmed by those who are seeking to end sexism, heterosexism, and racism.[5] Instead of keeping our attention on the women, the gays,

5 In a recent newspaper article, Philosophy Professor Carlos Prado wrote, "More and more university professors are being silenced by charges of racism, sexism and intolerance of cultural differences. Claims of academic freedom and freedom of expression fail to carry much weight against these charges" (Prado 1998).

lesbians and bisexuals, and the people of colour who are the targets of discrimination, the focus of attention ends up back where it's always been: on promoting the best interests of those who already enjoy significant privileges. And those who challenge those privileges are then cast in the role of supposedly repressive bad guys.

This move in the political correctness controversy also vastly overestimates the power of those who are protesting against inequality. For the supposed battle about political correctness at the present time is a very uneven one since those complaining the loudest about the alleged evils of feminists and other progressives have the force of the status quo and tradition on their side, and the ones they are complaining about are those who are daring to challenge political orthodoxy. Women who reject sexism are not operating on a so-called "level playing field" with men; gays, lesbians, and bisexuals who criticize straight privilege are subjected to harassment and assault that heterosexuals never face; and people of colour who challenge racism are subjected to a redoubling in racist persecution from the champions of white privilege.

Thus, giving umlimited free speech significant moral precedence over other values in the academy can produce a paradoxical outcome. Historically, the promotion of unrestricted free speech in institutions such as universities has frequently created restrictions on free speech for some people, in particular those who belong to groups subjected to systemic discrimination. If speech is so free that people are able to make statements in public forums that are sexist, racist, or homophobic, that "freedom" compromises the free speech of those persons who stand to be harmed by sexist, racist, or homophobic comments. Consider, for example, any professor whose professional work is founded upon sexist beliefs about the capacities and intelligence of women. What does protecting this man's free speech do to the potential free speech of the women who may have to sit in his classes, serve with him on committees, or perform secretarial work for him?

You have to almost admire a system sneaky enough to try to induce us to monitor each other's behaviour, and then to blame us for supposedly policing each other *and* our oppressors. But I take some comfort from my suspicion that the extent of the political, academic, and media outcry against the so-called "politically correct movement" (Fennell 1991, 41) is some indication both of the fear that progressive movements are invoking within conservative, repressive regimes and of the success that such movements are now achieving.

Nevertheless, feminists should be suspicious of the social uses and moral implications of the concept of political correctness as a motivator of role muddles. Policing each other with cries of "not PC" can be destructive: of ourselves, of community, of change. It represents no real departure from our patriarchally-assigned roles. As Marge Piercy (1990, 26) points out,

> The urge to be politically correct is best applied gently. It is well and wise to examine one's choices and actions, but policing other people is something women as mothers, as aunts, as teachers, as custodians of 'the way it ought to be' have functioned under patriarchy very long and very busily doing.

Having (barely) rescued ourselves from essentialism with respect to women, we had better not fall into it with respect to feminism. Narrow definitions of what constitutes politically correct feminism are inconsistent with both sides of the tension in feminism articulated by Snitow and other feminist theorists, inconsistent both with "articulating women's voice" and with "deconstructing gender" (Ferguson 1991, 322). For a univocal feminism is inconsistent with the existence of many and diverse women's voices, and the reifying of feminism is inconsistent with the constructed nature of gender. Feminist role muddles cannot be resolved merely by reference to standards of political correctness.

Some Non-Conclusions

How can I handle my feminist role muddles?

My aim in this discussion has been neither to characterize all the possible forms that feminist role muddles may take, nor to argue for my own particular version of feminism (which is still in the process of being worked out). Instead, I want to suggest the outlines of another method of responding to role muddles. Over the last few years I have figured out several steps I can take. While I don't want to imply that they solve the whole problem or that I always succeed in doing these things, when I do they are often effective.

First, I must recognize and acknowledge that none of us is infallible and we all make mistakes. As scholars and social activists, feminist academics need to be able to disagree, to reassess, to criticize. These processes enable our thinking and our strategies to grow and mature. If we can't make mistakes, it will be harder for us to learn.

From my work in peer counselling I have learned that what is sometimes most appropriate is just to listen when students, faculty, or administration—feminists and non-feminists alike—express their distress about feminists and feminism. Some of the disputes about feminism and political correctness are the expression of people's simultaneous longings for progressive social change and their resistance to and fear of such change. Instead of letting others arouse my own ever-ready feelings of feminist inadequacy, awkwardness, and moral compulsion, I can refuse to engage in mutual hand-wringing and despair, but instead just listen in an attentive and non-judgmental way, saving the expression of my own feelings until I find a safe and receptive listener.

Second, I can seek to disaffiliate from the privileges I now receive as a white, middle-class academic and reject the internalized oppression that helps to keep me divided from other women and other feminists. I can heed Marilyn Frye's wise observation (1992, 34) that

> [T]he integrity of a feminist working within ... an [anti-woman] institution must depend on her alienation from it and the constancy of her adversary relation with it. This orientation is maintained, not negatively through resistance of temptation or a system of coercive pressures and checks from other feminists, but positively, through woman-loving.

Genuinely caring about other women, as Frye advocates, particularly those who, as students, "support" staff, women of colour, and working-class women, do not share my privileges, is effective at least partly because it is incompatible with the distance and alienation that those privileges aim to promote.

Third, I can continue to rethink notions of political correctness. I can acknowledge, take responsibility for, and disaffiliate from my own participation in the evocation of notions of political correctness. I must learn to live with and sustain the tension between wanting to "know for sure" what feminism is (and is not) and the ambiguity and uncertainty necessitated by the openness and social power of this political and moral concept. It is a matter of seeing the line between mutual support and over-protection; of telling the truth, knowing there are many truths, and recognizing the constructed nature of (social) truth. We do have to keep defining ourselves, yet we must also be wary of the potential dangers of defining ourselves too narrowly.

As an alternative to politically and morally restrictive definitions of feminism, Kirsten Backstrom (1990, 11, 17) suggests that we see feminists as mavericks or "rogues":

> When men determine the standard…, any independent woman is a rogue. Any feminist, any lesbian, any woman of color is some sort of rogue…. A rogue is a woman who challenges assumptions. Any rigid definition is dangerous. If you can't change, you won't survive…. Her uniqueness arises from contradictions; she is not always right. Her motives are selfish and selfless. She is more than the sum of her parts.

While as feminists we can continue to aspire to high moral standards, we can also unashamedly refuse to be good, where "good" means conformity to norms we did not create.

Instead of attacking each other, or wallowing in self-conscious guilt, we can direct our anger and our power at

the conditions and institutions that create the competition and constraints that help to generate feminist role
muddles. As journalist Joanne Page (1990, 2) says, "In my
view, the enemy is the historical structure of society[,]
not a politically incorrect woman or man. Sure, we need
to change, men and women both. In order to do this, we
must embrace each other[,] not check credentials; we
need friends more than we need to be right." Especially,
I would add, since "being right" continues to be a matter
of complex and ongoing moral and political negotiation.

CHAPTER 3

Women and Men in Education

What would make me qualified to write about women and men in education? I can come up with only one answer: I am a woman who lives with men and who works with women and men—mostly men, in fact—within academia. I have also been teaching women and men for a number of years—for long enough that my son, who was a newborn near the beginning of my postsecondary teaching career, is now the age of my students. So whatever "expertise" or "authority" I may have on this topic comes not so much from scholarly research and qualifications as from that basic feminist resource, personal experience. I write, then, from the perspective of my experience as a female instructor, as well as my experiences as a former student (a long time ago!). But above all, I write, of course, from my perspective as a woman—a white, middle-class, middle-aged woman who has been fortunate enough to find herself part of that small minority of women who are members of academic communities.

It is obvious that a feminist would have lots to say about the situation of women, but why would a feminist want to write about men as well? As Mariah Burton Nelson points out,

> Feminists devote their attention to women. Thus stifled
> voices are amplified, as they should be. But to ignore
> men ... is to lose the opportunity to understand gender
> as ... a 'relational' process, a dynamic between men and
> women 'within a system of structured social inequality.'
> (Nelson 1991, 17)

I am convinced that there is much for feminists to learn
from both women and men about gender and about
inequality. In this chapter I shall therefore be quoting
occasionally not only from women but from men who are
investigating gender issues as they pertain to education.

Since I have been as much shaped and constrained as
anyone else by the social system that defines what it is to
be a woman and to be a man, I find that when I try to
think creatively about women and men in education I am
at the farthest limit of my imagination. So in this chapter what I shall partly be describing are ideals, ideals that
I can't myself claim that I always attain to. So sweeping
is the topic, "women and men in education," that to fully
explore it would require re-imagining the entire educational system, including all the other hierarchies—such
as government/university, instructor/student, and facul-
ty/staff—of which it is comprised.

And of course I cannot undertake to do all of that in
this chapter; there is no way for me to say everything that
needs to be said on this topic. I am not, for example,
going to discuss the sociology of women and men in education: the statistics that record the relative proportions
of women and men in various areas of study and instruction, the documentation of inequality and injustice, the
studies of interactions between women and men in
academic settings, and so on. Nor am I going to say a

great deal about how to make the university a better place specifically for women—though not surprisingly I take that project to be of the first importance. Such a project would include, at least minimally, safety, security, and freedom from sexual harassment for women on campus; good childcare for the offspring of faculty, staff, and students; support for mothers whether as students, faculty, or staff; the hiring of women in areas where their numbers are small; real respect for women staff; improvements in salaries and career opportunities; genuine backing of women's studies and scholarship in feminism; the presence of more women at higher levels of administration; the active recruiting of women students, especially in unrepresented fields; an end to homophobia and lesbophobia in academia; and probably many other steps I have not thought of.

But instead of discussing these areas, what I am going to present is a series of connected reflections about the gender-related values and practices—and some alternatives to them—that both compel and constrain women and men in education—primarily in university education, though I hope that some of what I say will apply to other educational levels as well. I think that there is much to be critical of, and also plenty to be hopeful about.

Some Theoretical Background

As a framework for the proposals I make later in this chapter, I shall start with some theoretical background about women and men in education, a background which

I can only sketch out here without fully developing it or offering complete evidence for it.

First, I assume that all human beings, and especially young human beings, are potentially if not actually intelligent, cooperative, loving, and enthusiastic beings. If people do not act that way, it is because they have been hurt in some manner, hurt, for example, through the operation of oppression. I also assume that all students, staff, and instructors in the educational system, no matter how they may sometimes appear, are full and real people, that they are much more than just the roles they play in the classroom, in the office, or in the cafeteria.

At the same time, I am highly suspicious of those versions of essentialism that ascribe inherent characteristics to women and to men on the basis of biological sex differences. My first hypothesis with respect to issues concerning women and men is always that the issues primarily involve social rather than just biological factors. Before ascribing apparently sex-linked characteristics to inherent physiological causes, it seems reasonable to first consider the role of socialization. The main reason for this approach is, of course, that there is now so much evidence about the cultural production of gender.

The concept of gender is central to feminists' understanding of women and men. Gender is femininity and masculinity, the cultural interpretation and elaboration of sex difference. It is the result of processes of socialization, the social construction that creates women and men. Gender could be described as a sexual ideology made flesh: our gender is expressed in how we dress, how we walk, how we talk (or don't talk; I'll return to that point), how we hold our bodies, think, moralize, work, and play. Gender is imprinted so deeply within our persons as to be invisible; we assume (falsely, I believe) that our gender just is us, that it constitutes us as human beings. And indeed, gender categories are deeply formative. Yet it is important to remember that gender is learned, not innate, that ways of sitting, speaking, thinking, and so on, are acquired, usually very early on, through the quite thorough cultural tutelage of institutions such as the media and persons such as parents, teachers, and schoolmates.

The rigidity and intensification of gender categories are closely related to the homophobia and lesbophobia that are attached to the social categories of sexual orientation. The persecution of lesbians, gay men, and bisexuals is at least partially a product of the attempt to obliterate any appearance of the so-called "masculine" in women and the "feminine" in men, to preserve the notion that women and men are naturally and inevitably very different. As Lynne Segal points out, this persecution "is a way of keeping men separated off from women, and keeping women subordinate to men" (Segal 1990, 16).

Robert Scholes has said that gender categories "allow no abstentions" (Scholes 1987, 206); that is, gender socialization does not permit much refusal to be a woman or to be a man in the social rather than biological senses of those terms. Yet it is possible to engage in what some have called "negotiations" about how gendered we will be; that is, what aspects of gender socialization we will accept and which we will reject. I referred earlier to the apparent depth of gender—yet paradoxically I would also insist upon its superficiality. Although I assume gender is socially constructed, I do not assume that its cultural determination makes individuals helpless. We can participate in our own self-creation; and as we become aware of the process, we can also choose to resist, reject, and reshape aspects of our genderization.[1]

Because the gender system encourages an emphasis on the differences between femininity and masculinity, it makes us lose sight of human similarities. My point here is not that women and men are all the same, that women must become (like) men, or that there is some neutral, non-gendered or androgynous "human being." But I am thinking here of Gayle Rubin's statement in her land-mark paper on "The Traffic in Women":

> Men and women are, of course, different. But they are not as different as day and night, earth and sky, yin and yang, life and death. In fact, from the standpoint of nature, men and women are closer to each other than either is to anything else—for instance, mountains, kangaroos, or coconut palms. (Rubin 1975, 179).

The gender categories of femininity and masculinity also assume and even coerce uniformity within the cate-gories. But of course all women are not alike; all men are not alike. In fact, taking into account differences in per-sonality, talents, physical capacities, and intelligence there is probably as much variation within the category of men and within the category of women as there is between the two categories. Recent feminist scholarship has rightfully encouraged deep suspicions about general-izing about women and men as groups and has drawn attention to the significant differences—most of them also the result of social construction—among members of the two gender categories resulting from differences in

---

1 Cf. Alcoff 1988, 434.

age, race, class, ability, and sexual orientation. When feminists criticize the limitations that are set by the norms of gender conformity, ironically we are often falsely interpreted by anti-feminists as saying that human beings should not be different from each other. Yet feminists are actually engaged in calling attention to the real differences among human beings, in spite of the requirements levied by the gender system.

Educational institutions have made some progress from the days when courses and training programs were assigned on the basis of people's sex. Yet even in classrooms and offices where gender appears to be irrelevant, relationships within educational institutions are largely about gender: they manifest the results of gender enculturation, and they are often founded upon unconfirmed beliefs in inherent sexual differences. The easy and appealing view of women and men in education would be that gender differences are inevitable, in academia, as anywhere else, but are benign or at least insignificant and that any difficulties between women and men are the result of misunderstandings which can be resolved through existing modes of education. But, as Adrienne Rich has persuasively suggested,

> If there is any misleading concept, it is that of 'co-education': that because women and men are sitting in the same classrooms, hearing the same lectures, reading the same books, performing the same laboratory experiments, they are receiving an equal education. They are not, first because the content of education itself validates men even as it invalidates women. Its very message is that men have been the shapers and thinkers of the world, and that this is only natural....

[In addition,] [w]omen and men do not receive an equal education because outside the classroom women are perceived not as sovereign beings but as prey. (Rich 1985, 24-25)

The university is in fact primarily a male institution, the site of what some feminists have called "masculinism." According to sociologist Arthur Brittan, masculinism is

the ideology that justifies and naturalizes male domination.... Masculinism takes it for granted that there is a fundamental difference between men and women, it assumes that heterosexuality is normal, it accepts without question the sexual division of labour, and it sanctions the political and dominant role of men in the public and private spheres.... In general, masculinism gives primacy to the belief that gender is not negotiable.... (Brittan 1989, 4)

Oppression is the systematic mistreatment of and injustice to a group through the cultural attitudes, economy, political system, and actions of individuals, groups, or institutions. In that variety of oppression called sexism, being female, and being socialized into the feminine gender, are made into a socially-constructed liability. The system of male dominance is defined in terms of violence and sexual access to women and entitlement to the services of women. Thinking clearly about women and men in education requires a recognition that sexual oppression is real and a full awareness of what is done to women in the name of male dominance. Sexual harassment, currently a high-profile issue at some universities, is just one example of the expression of male dominance and the masculinist expectation of sexual access to and service from women.[2]

Are men also oppressed? Individual men may be oppressed on the basis of their sexual orientation, their class, their race, their disability, or their religion, but they are not oppressed as men. For in the system of male dominance, reinforced by masculinism, being male is socially constructed as an asset, not a liability. "Being male is something [a man] has going *for* him, even if race or class or age or disability is going against him" (Frye 1983, 16, her emphasis). Nevertheless, although men are not, in my view, oppressed as men, they are subjected to a number of hurts on the basis of their sex, hurts having to do with gender requirements that demand enforced aggressiveness, participation in violent activity, and diminished or limited emotional expressivity. As Joseph Litvak puts it, "heterosexual masculinity is not an identity that one simply has, but an identification that one must be terrorized into" (Litvak 1995, 21).

---

2 When I was a graduate student, sexual harassment was a normal and accepted hazard of being female in academia. Everyone knew which male professors and graduate students were sexual predators. However, it was a hazard that had no name and was seen solely as the problem of the individual woman. For example, when I experienced repeated unwanted sexual advances from another graduate student, I planned carefully so as not to have to sit next to him in class. I regarded the situation as my own responsibility, not as the culpable behaviour of someone who should have kept his hands to himself and certainly not as an issue about which the university should have any concern. It was only years later, when the term "sexual harassment" was introduced into the feminist lexicon, that I recognized and understood what I had endured.

I assume that the oppression of women is in no way an inherent expression of men as human beings, that no men would participate in the oppression of women if they had not first been hurt in various ways, primarily as children, and that male dominance is a learned form of behaviour. Hence, men can, and sometimes do, choose to renounce the ideology of masculinism, and not to participate in the system of male dominance. Such a renunciation can be difficult, in part because male dominance is a component of the cultural definition of masculinity. This means that a man who ceases to participate in the oppression of women may often be regarded as less than fully masculine, less than fully a man. (Similarly, I would add, a woman who stops being a victim, who resists oppression, is often perceived to be not a real woman.) And although men can choose not to engage in oppressive behaviours, as men they still receive certain privileges accorded to members of their sex. As literary critic Stephen Heath remarks, "[H]owever many feminist women I know, it is not going to remove me from the structures of sexism, absolve me from the facts of male positioning, domination and so on" (Heath 1987a, 10).

Women and men therefore have somewhat different stakes in resisting sexism. The system of male dominance appears to be in men's interests at least in the sense that if there is going to be a limited amount of service, nurturance, power, money, jobs, and so on, available, then it is better to belong to the gender class that gets them. However, such a "benefit" is defined within existing social inequalities and scarcities. As complete, loving, peaceful human beings, seeking close, supportive, and flourishing relationships with women, male dominance is not in men's interests. To assume that men inherently desire to dominate and enjoy dominating women is to buy into an essentialist conception of men as innately oppressive beings who enjoy power over other human beings. That view is a counsel of despair with respect to the ending of social inequalities; it is virtually incapable of explaining the existence of men who reject and resist domination; and I believe it is completely false.

Some Proposals

With this set of background assumptions sketched out, I shall now outline a series of four proposals about the pragmatics of women and men in education. In what follows, I shall be highly critical of masculinism, the ideology of male domination, and of some aspects of masculinity as they are manifested within academia. While I also believe that there is much that is problematic about femininity, I do not think that femininity has a grip upon educational institutions—at least those at the university level—in the way and to the extent that masculinity surely does.

My criticisms should not necessarily be interpreted as a critique of men as individuals. As my later discussion will show, while I am critical of masculinism, and somewhat pessimistic about masculinity, I think there are reasons for optimism about men as persons! Nevertheless, much of what I say will be directed toward proposing steps not so much for women as for men to take to change the situation of women and men in education. This is largely because I believe that so much emphasis has already been placed on women's work for gender change; members of disadvantaged social groups are often considered to be the only persons responsible for working to end social injustices. It is surely time for more men to take up these responsibilities.

LISTENING

Communication is the life-blood of education. My first proposal is concerned with paying attention and listening. As feminist theorist Ann Snitow remarks,

> when women speak *as women* they run a special risk of not being heard because the female voice is by our culture's definition that-voice-you-can-ignore. But the alternative is to pretend that public men speak for women or that women who speak inside male-female forums are heard and heeded as much as similarly placed men. (Snitow 1990, 13, her emphasis)

Understanding and interpreting one's social reality and one's personal experience requires the conversational space to assemble one's thoughts and to speak or write at length about one's own views, without fear of interruption, and without the necessity of monitoring and even facilitating others' ongoing reactions. In most conversations and discussions, however, that space is not always available equally to everyone. There is plenty of research (for example, in Dale Spender's book, *Man Made Language* [1985]) to suggest that often women just are not listened to, are not permitted to expatiate at any length on their own ideas, yet are expected to keep the male stream of thought going—and are punished if they fail to fill that role. Spender says:

It is the *silence* of women, in language and in the use of language, that has emerged when women are considered in the patriarchal order....

Framing questions in terms of the silence of women leads to an examination of the language which excludes and denigrates them, and it also leads to an examination of their access to discourse. When the only language women have debases us and when we are also required to support male talk, it is not unlikely that we shall be relatively silent. When the only language men have affords them the opportunity to encode meanings and to control discourse, when they have made the language and decreed many of the conditions for its use, it is not unlikely that they will use it more and that they will use it more in their own interest; thus they assist in the maintenance of women's silence. (Spender 1985, 51, her emphasis)

Under these circumstances, it is not at all surprising that many women have a hard time developing the ability or grabbing the opportunity to present and give reasons for their views, but do learn the feminine skills of nurturing and fostering conversations conducted by men. And these *are* real skills. Unreflectively, we tend to believe that listening is just a matter of keeping our ears open and not falling asleep while someone talks, but in fact there is much more involved in really listening. Many people—not all of them men—have never learned to really listen, and some others—not all of them women—have never really learned to talk. Both of these skills are worth cultivating. I am convinced that there is a lot to be learned by "just" listening—listening, that is, without waiting for a tiny pause in which to inject one's own brilliant words. There is even more to be learned from the experience of "thinking out loud" while being listened to attentively, without the need to react, to entertain, or to defend oneself from "attack."

The operating assumption here is that the placing of attention can be a significant means for both moral growth and political change. Marilyn Frye puts it this way:

> Attention is a kind of passion. When one's attention is on something, one is present in a particular way with respect to that thing....

> The maintenance of phallocratic reality requires that the attention of women be focused on men and men's projects—the play; and that attention not be focused on women—the stagehands. (Frye 1983, 172)

We have to actually notice, to recognize, to truly see people, and to hear what they have to say, before we are able to understand their experience, to acknowledge their needs and purposes, and to support their goals. Receiving the recognition and attention of others is essential for the development of a sense of oneself and one's own capacity for knowing and understanding. Being listened to is especially important with respect to people such as children, women, people of colour, and people with disabilities, who for political reasons are less visible within this culture—or, if they are visible, to whom the rule of "seen but not heard" is usually applied.

And because the skills of listening are both valuable and undervalued, they should not continue to be assigned exclusively to members of the female sex. When I first got a university job, I noticed that at academic and social events there was very little listening going on. Within that mostly-male environment, many individuals did a lot of talking, but they gave relatively little genuine attention to each other's speech—except perhaps in an effort to refute threatening statements. I suspect that one of the many ways in which the growing presence of women has enriched the university environment is through women's capacities to listen and to provide a receptive audience. But these capacities are in no way inevitably sex-linked. It is possible for academics of either sex to learn and to model real listening.

Instructors can also cultivate the practice of listening within their students. While there are obviously some limits on what instructors can do in their teaching insofar as they cannot make the classroom entirely a refuge from the effects of oppression, instructors can at least make the classroom a place where open thinking and expression of differing experiences and opinions are possible. Women's studies scholar Barbara Hillyer Davis suggests that the function of the instructor can be compared to that of a "simultaneous translator." She says:

> This role involves hearing and giving back in other words what another person has just said, and at the same time presenting an explanation in another language which will illuminate the issue for a second group without alienating the first. (Davis 1985, 250)

It is essential for instructors to model complete respect, genuine interest in others, and a willingness to listen, along with no tolerance for the expression of sexism or other forms of discrimination such as racism or homophobia.

One way to cultivate listening skills in students is to set aside time in class in which people have the opportunity to take turns both listening and speaking, by dividing up the time equally within a pair or a small group of people. In real listening the listener does not interrupt; does not make "helpful" comments; does not prompt in any way; does not offer sympathy, commiseration, personal stories, or judgments; but simply listens in a relaxed, attentive, interested manner, maintaining eye contact wherever possible. If the talker runs out of things to say, or prefers silence while "her time" is still running, the listener should just wait in respectful, expectant silence. After half the time, the two roles of talker and listener are switched.

If part of the goal is to enhance communication between women and men, it may be necessary to take some risks with the usual classroom protocol in which the eager beavers do most of the talking. One possibility is the classic "go round" in which everyone is offered the opportunity to speak about a particular topic. Another is to institute a practice in which no one speaks twice until everyone has spoken once. You can even try occasionally offering the opportunity to members of one affinity group—such as women—to be listened to with interest and respect by the members of the other group—in this case, men. The members of the group can be invited to talk about such things as what is good about belonging to that group, what is hard about it, what they want others to know about them, what kinds of support they need, and what they never want to hear said about them again.

When genuine listening is introduced into a classroom or a meeting, some hard things may be said. In particular, when women are given the opportunity to talk, they may utter some truths about their experience that are painful for men to hear. It is essential for men not to interpret what they may hear from women as nothing more than individual attack, blame, or reproach, or as an attempt to silence men. While listening to descriptions of women's oppression may be hard for men, experiencing that oppression has been even harder for women. Giving half of the conversational air space to women may feel like "silencing" to people who have always enjoyed the monopoly on listening, but in fact it is simple justice. The equalization of the balance of attention may turn out to be a challenge for some men, but real listening can also be rewarding, for there is so much that can be learned from it. Here, for example, is what one man, Craig Jones, at the time a graduate student at Queen's University, learned from genuinely listening to women:

> [L]et it be recognized *as fact* that throughout their lives, women are in greater danger from men than they are from *any other source*. Women don't fear by choice, no woman makes a decision to fear men. There is no policy among feminists to fear men. Fear of men is a *fact* of many women's lives, a fact that derives from either direct personal—often extremely painful—experience or from the irrefutable knowledge that the odds are high that eventually they will be violated or harassed or assaulted in some manner by a man. (Jones 1990, 15, his emphasis)

Jones says that recognizing this aspect of women's lives was painful for him, but I think there can be little doubt about the depth of thought and the motive to understand that lies behind his description of what he has heard from women.

I should stress that I am not just saying that now the tables must be turned, and men must only listen to women, never expressing their own perspectives. It seems highly likely that women will also continue to listen to men, but both women and men will learn more about each other if men sometimes change the way they speak. It is almost a truism to say that women would welcome more genuine self-disclosure and intimacy from men. In fact, in the interests of understanding the workings of sexism and the nature of gender enculturation, it is especially important for men to talk about how the ideology of masculinity is experienced by men. As an example, here is what one man, a native American named Medicine Story, had to say to women about his life as a man. He asked women to imagine themselves as the targets of the gender requirements usually directed at men:

> [A]sk yourselves what it might be like if you were in a society where women subjugated men and how it would feel to be seen as tyrants by the men you wanted to become close to? What would it be like if women, in the name of their womanhood, had to go out and kill other women? What would it be like if from infancy you were taught it was unwomanly to weep or show your grief? What would it be like if you could not touch or get close to other women? What would it be like if the only intimacy society approved of were sexual, if it were unwomanly to be affectionate or tender? What would it

be like if you were taught that your functions were to assume all responsibility, make all decisions, never be wrong, and work to provide for all your family's requirements, incidentally supplying occasional seed for reproduction? (Story 1989, 50)

Clearly, there is much that both women and men can learn from a man who speaks out about his own experience of masculinity.

THE CULTURE OF THE CLASSROOM

The relationships between women and men in education may be changed if we reassess some aspects of masculine ideology that seem to pervade some classrooms: competition, adversarial relations, and lack of emotion, limited range of emotion, or inability to deal with emotion.

Feminist philosopher Janice Moulton has proposed the reevaluation of a phenomenon within academia that she calls "the unhappy conflation of aggression with success." She says:

Aggression may have no causal bearing on competence, superiority, power, etc., but if many people believe aggressive behavior is a sign of these properties, then one may have to learn to behave aggressively in order to appear competent, to seem superior, and to gain or maintain power. (Moulton 1989, 6)

Moulton suggests that we reject what she calls "the adversary method" that seems to govern much university education: a model that sees classroom interaction as competition, complete with attackers and defenders, winners and losers, and the monopoly on truth awarded to those who are most combative. Academia is rife with metaphors of attack and defend, advance and undermine—metaphors that are, I believe, a part of the ideology of masculinity. This doctrine of combat and opposition is exacerbated by the recent introduction into academia of market metaphors. Both external observers and university administrators themselves routinely speak of "intellectual capital," "investments" (in students or faculty), "market accountability," and the academic "bottom line."

Thus, much of the educational process is founded upon conflict and competition—not only competition among educational institutions, but also among students and even implicit competition between instructor and students. Years ago a colleague of mine pointed out to me that instructors often set themselves up as what he called "the smartest kid in the class." You know the sort of thing: the instructor asks a question, a few of the bravest students take a try at answering it, they all get it wrong, and then the teacher—surprise, surprise—comes out with the correct response.

My scepticism about pedagogical competition does not imply that I think that disagreement and contention are inevitably bad or should be avoided; in fact controversy and reasoned argument are often the source of considerable learning. But what is troublesome is the assumption of scarcity that underlies much academic controversy: that there is only a little intelligence or talent or correct thinking to go around; that some have it and others don't; and that truth can be discovered, or even won, through a competitive process in which all but one of the combatants will be defeated.

Partly as a result of these implicit operating assumptions about limited truth, intelligence, and correct thinking, praise and validation are also in short supply in education. Because of the scarcity assumption many people have the suspicion that if one person is doing well, then the rest of us can't be. Most instructors have a pattern of writing criticisms and corrections all over student papers, but are somewhat less likely to recognize and applaud what is good in students' work. The lack of validation goes the other way too. As instructors everywhere know, students are quick to criticize bad teaching, but are sometimes less forthcoming in rewarding good teaching. Stinginess about validation is a product of the adversarial method: after all, if students are in competition with each other, and in competition with the instructor, then no one is going to be too liberal in appreciating a competitor.

I'm suggesting, then, that the situation of women and men in education might be improved if we were to reevaluate some aspects of the culture of the classroom that are shaped by masculine ideology, including competition, adversarial relations, the assumption of scarcity, and the failure to validate.

I think we also need to reassess the place of emotion in education. The discrediting of emotion so characteristic of western thought and of the practical operation of most institutions in North America is related to the discrediting of women, since identifying, feeling, expressing, and understanding emotions is usually assigned to the female gender, not the male. Lack of emotional expressiveness—beyond the fairly familiar emotions of hostility and anger—is a way of maintaining control and dominance, because it permits the concealment of personal vulnerabilities. I suspect that many women's tendency to greater emotional expressiveness is also used, inappropriately, as part of the covert justification for failing to promote women into the higher reaches of academic administration.

Nevertheless, emotional expression need not be incongruent with thinking and reason. In fact, thoughtful processes of emotional discharge (for example, crying, trembling, or laughing) may facilitate thinking. From many of the students whom I have taught I've learned that emotions in the classroom—anxiety, sadness, anger, exhilaration, joy—are not always to be feared but often to be welcomed. For example, providing she receives a warm and receptive response, a student who may cry while describing her experiences of sexism or racism not only offers an intensely moving source of insight to the other students, but also has the opportunity to recover a bit from the harms she has sustained, and to learn to analyze them in greater depth.

It is important to aim for safety in the classroom, so that people feel reasonably secure and unthreatened. The seminar or lecture is not a free-for-all where "anything goes." In a classroom lecture on International Women's Day, during which I discussed the situation of women students and faculty in the university, a tall young man stood up, shook his fist at me, and proclaimed that it was women like me who were ruining his life. He may have just realized that he would no longer have automatic access to privileges on the basis of his sex. He was very angry, and I felt some fear. I endeavoured to listen patiently and confidently to his claims, and he soon subsided. But I do not believe that students of either sex should be encouraged or even permitted to wield their feelings as a means of intimidation. I am not willing to tolerate expressions of emotion that overwhelm or undermine me or my students.

While safety is essential, it may not always be possible to create emotional comfort[3] in the classroom. But discomfort, itself, can be a source for new approaches and reassessments of old ways of thinking. I am encouraged in this view by philosopher Alison Jaggar, who has described the role of what she calls "outlaw emotions"— that is, those emotions that are conventionally unacceptable (Jaggar 1989, 144)—as a source of new insight: for example, pride in women's accomplishments; anger at a sexist comment; laughter at the pretensions of those who wield power; and grief rather than vanity or patriotism over the destruction and violence resulting from a so-called "just war." Jaggar says:

> When certain [outlaw] emotions are shared or validated by others ... the basis exists for forming a subculture defined by perceptions, norms, and values that systematically oppose the prevailing perceptions, norms, and values. By constituting the basis for such a subculture, outlaw emotions may be politically (because epistemologically) subversive. (Jaggar 1989, 144)

In general, for those who are committed to challenging oppression and ending the ideology of masculinism, there may be much to be gained from redefining the culture of the classroom.

---

3 In Chapter 4 I describe my experience with a class where the distinction between safety and comfort became crucial to my pedagogy.

RESISTING INTERNALIZED
OPPRESSION AND INVALIDATION

As women and men in education we all need to become aware of and to reject internalized oppression and internalized invalidation. According to Sandra Bartky, "Something is 'internalized' when it gets incorporated into the structure of the self" (Bartky 1988, 77). One of the ways in which oppressive systems are particularly effective is by training us to police ourselves (Bartky 1988, 80), to accept and to actively apply within our own personal spheres the social norms of invalidation and discrimination. Internalized oppression and invalidation may be directed against oneself—as when a woman believes that she herself is less able because she is a woman; or it may be directed against other members of one's group as a manifestation of "horizontal hostility"—as when a woman assumes that other women must inevitably be weak, unintelligent, or unsuited to leadership positions. Internalized oppression is manifesting itself in women when they do not expect the best from themselves and from each other in terms of leadership, intellectual achievements, or physical strength and agility. Similarly, while caring has been an often valuable component of traditional femininity, when women students, staff, and faculty take all the responsibility for nurturance, counselling, and caring, and direct that caring primarily at men, they are manifesting internalized oppression. I believe that women need to focus more on mutual support and on refusing to set limits on each other, rather than on worrying about caring for the men around us.

Similarly, internalized invalidation is manifesting itself in men when they do not expect the best from themselves and from each other in terms of emotional depth, support, and understanding, or when they go along with the idea that it is manly to use pornography, to harass and coerce women, or to engage in threats and aggression. Stephen Heath suggests that men should begin the process of understanding gender "by trying to grasp *who we are as men*" (Heath 1987b, 45, his emphasis). I hope that men will start taking and reclaiming pride in who they really are as individual, unique human beings who happen to be male. Just as women have been starting to take pride in being women, maybe men need to ask, what are we proud of as men? what, if anything, is positive about masculinity?

For members of both sexes, resisting internalized oppression and invalidation means not giving in to hope-lessness, whether about oneself, about other people of the same sex, or about members of the other sex. Giving up internalized invalidation means acknowledging that women are not just caregivers or victims, and that men are not just oppressors or guys who never get it right.

RESISTING SEXISM

My final proposal is the obvious one: that sexism in education must be interrupted and resisted. Resisting sexism in education involves, first, some basic steps, such as the avoidance of sexist and unnecessarily gendered language; the rejection of role stereotyping (who runs the audio-visual equipment? who makes the coffee?); the repudiation of sexist remarks and jokes; the prevention of sexual harassment and assault; and the insistence upon complete respect for all members of the academic community.

But in addition to these changes that feminists and pro-feminists have been proposing for years, I would like to suggest another partial goal: women and men perceiving themselves and acting as liberation allies to each other. What is an ally? Teacher Allen Levy suggests that an ally is a person who thinks and works with us, not for us. An ally doesn't necessarily expect our agreement. An ally is honest and genuine; an ally cares about us, not for us. An ally is a good listener, and an ally helps us to preserve and to develop far-reaching visions of what is possible, both within ourselves and within our society (Levy 1986, 48).

I know that many men in academia are ready to be allies of women in creating a non-sexist culture.[4] They have listened to feminists who have been stating for years that ending oppression is not just the job of members of the oppressed group, and that educating the oppressors is not the task of the oppressed. This means explicitly acknowledging and critiquing one's privileges and assuming leadership with respect to ending sexism. Good intentions of being non-sexist and declarations of support for women are not enough. But it does not mean that men should walk around feeling guilty for being male, or that men should step back and "let" women take

---

4 Some years ago a male faculty member invited me to consider him as an "honorary woman." At the time I was not impressed, believing that his invitation was an attempt to arrogate to himself the cozy intimacy women are thought to enjoy among themselves without, of course, his having to pay any of the costs associated with being gendered female. Now I take a more charitable interpretation: in a clumsy way, the man was offering his support and his willingness to try to understand what it means to be a woman in academia. I'd like to believe that he wanted to be an ally.

over. What is needed from men is not self-abasement but self-respect.

Being a male ally means doing some of the anti-sexist work, including sometimes the dull, boring, unheroic work—without "father knows best" attitudes or appropriating feminist projects. It means neither leaving women on their own, nor taking over. In this vein, the Ottawa branch of the anti-violence organization of men called "BrotherPeace" proposed the following anti-sexist actions for men: "challenge men's anger toward feminists; reject pornography; support lesbian and gay rights; speak out against sexist behaviour; take 'no' for an answer" (BrotherPeace 1990). In terms of specific academic measures, men can also be allies of women by reading women's writings, attending classes given by women, and choosing feminist topics for their assignments and research. Whether as students or instructors themselves, men can support, not protect, women students; refuse to exploit or condescend to women staff; advocate the promotion of women into administration; and act as mentors to women graduate students and new faculty.

In taking on this program, I would urge men not to expect and seek out congratulations and enormous praise for their efforts at opposing sexism—women should not have to do this kind of nurturing too. While validation is, as I have pointed out, an important aspect of human interaction, persons with privilege should not demand validation for repudiating some of their privileges. Instead, what women as allies can offer men is the willingness to look beyond negative masculine stereotypes; to recognize men as beings who are more than and other than sexual predators, economic kingpins, or physical threats; indeed, to see men as full human persons who are not so different from women.

If being a male ally in the ways I suggested earlier looks like a large burden for men, remember the burden that women carry as the targets of sexism. Stephen Heath expresses the paradoxes of men's responsibilities to end sexism in this way:

> Men have a necessary relation to feminism—the point after all is that it should change them too, that it should involve learning new ways of being women *and men* against and as an end to the reality of women's oppression—and that relation is also necessarily one of a certain exclusion—the point after all is that this is a matter *for women*, that it is their voices and actions that must determine the change and redefinition…. Which does not mean, of course not, that I can do nothing in my life, that no actions are open to me, that I cannot respond to and change for feminism…. (Heath 1987a, 1, his emphasis)

What I have been proposing, throughout this chapter, is a version of what Marilyn Frye calls "disaffiliation." Frye writes:

> Feminists make use of a distinction between being male and being 'a man,' or masculine. I have enjoined males of my acquaintance to set themselves against masculinity. I have asked them to think about how they can stop being men, and I was not recommending a sex-change operation. (Frye 1983, 127)

This process of setting oneself against masculinism and traditional masculinity is the process of disaffiliation. John Stoltenberg calls it "refusing to be a man" (Stoltenberg 1990). I suggest that it applies to women, too: women need to think about disaffiliating ourselves from the crippling aspects of femininity. Disaffiliation, in this sense, means not settling for limits on who we can be and what we can do, not settling for limits on who we are as human beings. I don't pretend that disaffiliation is simple; in fact, it's a disorienting, scary, and even paradoxical process. For I am simultaneously urging people both to disaffiliate from traditional gender expectations and requirements and also to claim and reclaim pride in themselves as human beings who happen to be female or male.

As a system of social categories, gender should provoke at least our ambivalence rather than our unthinking allegiance. While women may sometimes be valued, in academic settings, for their acculturated capacities for nurturance, listening, and mediating conflict, these characteristics are sometimes also used as a way of dismissing women for not being tough enough to handle the pressures and demands of the new university climate. As a result, some women are inclined to downplay typical gender-associated traits for the sake of conformity to the masculine norm, passing as male "wannabes." But neither passive gender conformity nor unthinking gender rejection offers a resolution to academic sexism.

Instead, I hope everyone in the university will think creatively about the situation of women and men in education. Education can be an important, indeed crucial, site for the subversion of sexism and the termination of masculinism. We don't need to accept oppression and powerlessness. We don't need to acquiesce in the fates that the ideologies of gender seem to foretell for us. We don't need to settle for limits on what we can do and what we can be. It is not only the integrity of our educational system that is at stake here; it is our humanity.

86

CHAPTER 4

A Tale of Two Classes

[T]he personal is a performance, an appearance contrived for the public, and ... these masks enable us to perform the play of pedagogy. (Grumet 1995, 37)

Although I am always a feminist academic, I am not always, while I teach, the same person. And although teaching is in some ways like acting, a performance as university instructor, I do not always play my part in the same way.

Nor should I. Each class in the academic year is like a new act in an ongoing play, or a new chapter in the history of my teaching. I am always at—or on—a new stage in my personal and professional life.

First as a music instructor, then as a philosophy professor, I have been teaching young people all my working life. When I started my teaching career my students were only a few years younger than me. But every year while I get older I confront a new crop of students, almost all of whom are in late adolescence or their early twenties. From my perspective it is like being caught in a time warp, where no one else ages except me.

Inevitably I find myself receding from my students. My cultural referents, the significant historical events of my youth—the death of US President Kennedy, the cult of the Beatles, Expo 67, the first moonwalk, the War Measures Act—happened long before these people were even born.

A true watershed was reached the first time one of my students said to me, "You remind me of my mother." As a feminist, I sincerely hoped this was a compliment: that the student had a good relationship with her mother, and something about my behaviour recreated that connection. Nonetheless, whether intended positively or negatively, the remark firmly fixed me: I could no longer even pretend to be within or near the generation of my students, but must resign myself to being of their parents' generation. Where once I was a not-yet-tenured assistant professor, now I am a tenured and secure full professor. Where once I was the mother of small children, now I am the mother of young people who are closer in age to my students than I am.

Just as I am never the same teacher, feminist though I always am, from one year to the next, I can't assume that the classes are the same. Not only are different classes composed of different individuals, but, less obviously, the collective personality of the classes change as the individuals who comprise them change. The moral views, political perspectives, educational goals, and personal needs of the class can be quite different among students who have, ostensibly, all chosen to study the same subject—and not only different from each other, but also different from year to year. David Crane writes:

> A class is a course embodied; it has a certain temporal, locational, dynamic, and personalized makeup. It has a specificity that cannot be duplicated no matter how many times the course is offered or taken, no matter how its story is told; it is a course caught in the act. (Crane 1995, xiii)

I learned this the hard way, by failing to recognize it and then being forced to acknowledge it. Almost every year since 1986 I have taught PHIL-375, "Philosophy and Feminism," a year-long third-year undergraduate seminar course. This is the story of what I learned from two different classes of PHIL-375, and how the students in the two groups transformed my approach to teaching. Like all cautionary tales, this story has a moral. I had to learn to play new pedagogical roles, and in the end what helped me was the evocation of the students' very different experiences.

Class One

In 1989-90 PHIL-375 had twenty-three students, all but one of whom were undergraduates in the second, third, and fourth years of their programmes. (The exception was a male first-year Masters student who audited the course.) Two-thirds of the class were women. All of the students were white. About one-third of the group came out in class or identified themselves privately to me as gay, lesbian, or bisexual. The students' academic backgrounds were primarily in philosophy and/or women's studies, but many were concentrating in other areas, notably drama, film studies, history, sociology, religion, and politics.

The credit for the ways in which this class evolved and matured from September, 1989, to April, 1990, largely belongs to the students, who persistently showed me that I could trust them to think well about the class and to experiment thoughtfully with new approaches to learning. They also challenged most of my notions of the "real" limits both of classroom propriety and of political achievement on campus. Classes were often rowdy, excited, full of feelings and talk. The students' extra-curricular political activities constantly surpassed my preconceived notions of what was possible on a white, middle-class, conservative, small-town campus.

The members of the class had a mixed bag of political values and goals. While for many, feminist work was the priority, others focused their political attention on such areas as peace activism, prison reform, animal rights, anti-racism, and anti-homophobia work. About a quarter of the class also reported and wrote for various campus publications, so that I used to say, with some bemusement, that three-quarters of the class were engaged in political activism and the other quarter were engaged in reporting on them.

Whereas many people have the idea that philosophy is necessarily an esoteric, remote, difficult, intellectual preoccupation with little or no connection to people's real concerns and lives, I am convinced that thinking about philosophical issues is something we all can and will do, if not systematically discouraged or mocked for doing so. Philosophical thinking is concerned with issues that centrally define and affect human beings, their perspectives on this universe, and their ways of being and acting in the world. I have heard children as young as five raise what I consider to be philosophical questions about topics relating to morality and spirituality, and children as young as nine consider issues in metaphysics and epistemology. The problem is, usually, that young children are discouraged from thinking and speaking philosophically by the reactions of adults: uncomprehending, mocking, or aggressively corrective. But with a receptive, interested, encouraging audience, the philosophical impulse, which is quintessentially human, can be reawakened and nurtured even within the minds of those who have survived the deadening impact of unimaginative child rearing or repressive schooling.

With these assumptions in mind, at the beginning of the year I set a few ground rules for the class. I pointed out that, by virtue of our institutional relationship, I could not divest myself of some forms of power over them, the power to determine their final grade being the most obvious of these. I told them that there were real skills I wanted them to develop, and that I would expect, anticipate, and encourage high levels of achievement in the class. Philosophy is learned by actively engaging in it, through speaking and writing about philosophical issues as much and as often as possible. I therefore told the class that I expected attendance in class, hoped for participation in class discussion, and required certain types of written work to be submitted.[1] I told them that some classes would be led by me and others by individual students: every student would present a seminar in each term, either alone or in tandem with another student, depending on their choice. Students were also expected to read the assigned readings I had tentatively outlined at the beginning of the term.[2] I said that no expressions of

1 Students were to write two short (3-4 pages) "position papers" and one seminar write-up in each term; they could choose to substitute a longer term paper for two of the position papers in one term. I also gave the students freedom, within each term, to choose when to submit their work, and what readings and topics on which to focus.

2 I assigned an ambitious and fairly difficult list of works in feminist philosophy (Frye 1983; Grimshaw 1986; Code, Mullet, and Overall 1988; and Griffiths and Whitford 1988), with the anticipation that we would discuss one or two readings per week.

racism, homophobia, or sexism would be tolerated in class, and that every class member was expected to listen with interest and respect when someone was speaking, and to refrain from attacking individuals.

I added (without knowing where this would take me) that when students were presenting their seminars, they could do so in any way they believed appropriate and effective, provided that the presentation examined the assigned reading for the day and stimulated thoughtful discussion among the class.

The challenges to my limited notions of appropriate classroom activities began almost immediately. Kirsten, a young woman who was a first-class philosophy major and a gifted dancer, had chosen to give the first seminar. It was based upon philosopher Marilyn Frye's paper, "Oppression," which uses a number of spatial metaphors to define and illuminate the mechanisms of oppression. Frye writes:

> the root of the word 'oppression' is the element 'press.'...Presses are used to mold things or flatten them or reduce them in bulk, sometimes to reduce them by squeezing out the gasses or liquids in them. Something pressed is something caught between or among forces and barriers which are so related to each other that jointly they restrain, restrict or prevent the thing's motion or mobility. Mold. Immobilize. Reduce. (Frye 1983, 2)

Kirsten asked if she could lead the group in some dance exercises as an introduction to discussion of the paper. She wanted the class to participate in movements that would enable us to experience being pressed, flattened, and molded.

I was dubious about her proposal; it sounded flaky, and I'd never seen anything like this happen in a Queen's University classroom. But her description of the rationale for this approach, and the light in her eyes, convinced me to take the risk[3] of saying yes—on the condition that a formal presentation would follow, which would develop some aspect of the reading on oppression and be linked to the dance exercises.

That seminar presentation turned out to be a landmark in my education as a teacher. Under Kirsten's gentle guidance we pushed the tables and chairs to the edges of the room. Filled with music, movement, colour, and sweaty bodies, animated by Kirsten's energetic, confident, light-hearted leadership, the class was a tremendous success. She had us move around upright, then imagine that the ceiling was descending upon us, gradually pressing us lower and lower to the floor. She had us try to resist the pressing ceiling, then gradually succumb to its power. The half hour of dancing was followed by two hours of intense, voluble, passionate discussion of oppression: what it is, who suffers from it, where it comes from, and how it can be resisted.

Kirsten's seminar presentation inspired and electrified the group. Her class set a creative precedent for the ensuing weeks, and virtually every meeting was different. Throughout the year we enjoyed a series of presentations that included listening to music, making posters, participatory theatre, writing together, excerpts from films,

---

3 Experimentation seemed especially risky to me because I was being considered for tenure that year.

completing questionnaires, producing art, small group discussions, and role-playing.

In one memorable class two women students led a lively discussion of feminist separatism by first defining the term and then leading the women to another room to continue the discussion. For the rest of the session, many of the women wrestled with their discomfort at having "abandoned" the men and with the moral and political implications of perhaps having "lost" some of their best allies. Meanwhile, the men (as I found out later) relaxedly discussed the reading amongst themselves and debated their own roles in feminist social change.

In another class, a film student showed a video she had made of a new mother exploring her perceptions of her baby and of motherhood, and then led a discussion of the notion, in feminist ethics, of "caring." In a discussion of white women's complicity in racism, one student distributed a very perceptive questionnaire which helped the class to focus on their unaware assumptions about race identification and privilege. In a class on women as epistemic authorities, the class sat in a circle and took turns describing a woman who was important in their lives and the kind of knowledge she had given them. In a session on the gay rights movement, lesbian and gay leaders in Kingston were invited to join the meeting to provide support to the lesbian, gay, and bisexual minority in the class. In a class on the ethics of self-abnegation, a woman student led a dialogue with her mother, whom she brought as a guest, on the nature of self-sacrifice. In a class that probed the prospects for future liberation, two students welcomed us to the "new world" we had just reached by "spaceship," then conducted us into a classroom where furniture had been pushed against the walls

and lights were dimmed. We sat on blankets and cush-
ions, shared light snacks, and were invited to devise and
discuss a new set of ethical and policy guidelines that
would obviate old forms of discrimination and injustice,
using principles of feminist ethics.

Meanwhile, my role in the classroom became a relatively minor one. I required that students tell me, in
advance, what they were planning to do in class; that the
activities must be related to the assigned reading for the
day; and that there had to be a short presentation with
group discussion which would link the reading, the activities, and the student's interpretation of them. My job
was to encourage creativity, be receptive to independent
thinking, and guide analysis.

The work the students produced was sometimes ordinary, but more often superb and inspiring. It was a class
where attendance was almost perfect and participation
was very high.

From that group I received a legacy that I carried to
future versions of "Philosophy and Feminism." I have to
acknowledge that it was my students who pushed me to
change. The only claim I can make for myself is that I
saw the benefits of change, recognized the resources that
students bring to the classroom, and was willing to support, encourage, and learn from innovation in my
students. So I now invite my students to consider how
they can give a presentation that will engage not only
students' minds, but also their muscles, their senses, their
aesthetic sensibilities, and their creative capacities.
I suggest they use the classroom as an opportunity to
grapple with the reality of the issues raised in the readings. I encourage, though I do not require, students to
work together in pairs, since I have learned that more

interesting and innovative interpretations often emerge from working with another person. I also found that if I go in with the expectation that students will be lively, interesting, highly motivated, and independent learners, then they usually are.

I still do a lot of work in terms of course planning and design. I lecture briefly about key concepts and claims. Much of my effort goes toward helping to teach students to be better writers. And I model some of the innovations in presentation that students might use.

My own predilection is for discussion and writing exercises. One such exercise is having students write, at or near the beginning of class, about an issue that we will be exploring, then have the students share the results of their writing either with one other student or with the whole group. Another is to have students line up across the length of the room, with each end of the room representing a different position with respect to a particular issue. This allows students to recognize and respect gradations of opinion, to see that one need not completely agree or completely disagree but can partially agree, partially disagree.

I don't want to suggest that the 1989-90 class from which I learned so much was easy to deal with. As a group they were often volatile, angry, and unpredictable, and I was often scared and uncomfortable during our classes. The political and social divisions in the class were explosive: they included female/male, heterosexual/lesbian, gay, bisexual; pro-choice/pro-life; radical feminist/reformist feminist; liberal/socialist/anarchist; and feminist/humanist. The class met twice a week; between meetings I sometimes didn't know all the things they had been up to, and I would come to class to find that feelings were running high about some brand new issue, or that they had taken on some new cause and were preoccupied with it.

I learned to acknowledge that they would likely have lots of feelings about the topics we covered and to state that I didn't think feelings should be banished from the classroom, that there were some errors on both sides in the traditional thinking/emotion dichotomy, and that people could often think better about difficult issues if they did not avoid or push away their feelings. We spent a couple of classes reading some feminist philosophical evaluations of emotions and reconsidering their possible connections to feminist thought and action.

As I watched this class develop and unfold, I found that they became a closely bonded group who supported and trusted each other. Throughout the year most members of the class engaged in extensive political activism across the spectrum of their commitments. My students often informed me ahead of time about their political plans, and fortunately I usually managed to refrain from expressing my pessimism about their chances of success. Based on my observations of their work, I no longer make assumptions about the potential limits of student activism.

There were some notable events. In the fall, a group of young men on campus had hung misogynous signs in the windows of their university residence. When the university administration refused to respond in any way, a group of women, including most of the female members of my class, occupied the office of the Principal for two days and a night, obtained nation-wide and sympathetic media coverage of the issues, and emerged with commitments from the administration to take concrete action on a range of women's concerns on campus. (Interestingly, a group of men, including some from my class, also kept a supportive vigil outside the building where the sit-in was held.)

Later in the year a group of students, including some from my class, attended the semi-annual meeting of the University's Board of Trustees and won from them an agreement to donate $10,000 to Kingston's over-extended Sexual Assault Crisis Centre, which is situated on campus, and to devote a day to educating them-selves, as a group, about the problem of sexual assault on campus.

When the federal Parliament was debating the possi-ble implementation of a restrictive new abortion law, a number of my students went to Ottawa, chained them-selves to the railings of the Visitors Gallery in the House of Commons, and showered pro-choice leaflets on the heads of astonished Parliamentarians.

These political events in particular stand out for me, but there were many others. My students engaged in extensive work on educating people about cruelty to ani-mals; assisting prison inmates to communicate with the "outside" world; opposing the marketing of war toys at Christmas time; forming activist campus groups to oppose racism and homophobia; and supporting native Canadians in their demands for recognition of land own-ership claims. The academic year was both intellectually exciting and politically productive. Feminist philosophy, personal experience, and political activism were mutually influential and integrated.

Class Two

In 1991-92, after gaining tenure and spending a year on sabbatical, I was again scheduled to teach "Philosophy and Feminism." I wanted to find out whether the students in PHIL-375 in 1989-90 were an exceptional group or whether, with new students, we could continue to create the conditions to enable intellectual growth, political change, and personal evolution to occur together.

This new group was superficially similar to the earlier one. Of the twenty-four second-, third- and fourth-year students, three-quarters were women. About a quarter of the class identified as gay, lesbian, or bisexual. All but three of the students were white. The students' academic backgrounds were diverse.

The 1991-92 group were active in university politics and involved in campus journalism. Enrolled in the class were the editor of a radical campus publication, her co-editor, a contributing columnist, and many supporters. The class included several queer activists and an outspoken mature student who subsequently became a campus student leader.

This group, however, was different in important ways from the group I'd had in 1989-90. Many of the students were aggressive, outspoken, and angry. The others—those not active in politics or journalism—were quiescent, and they were often on the receiving end of the active ones' anger.

As the term unfolded the atmosphere of the class became more and more disturbed. It seemed that nothing could be said, including by me, that did not outrage somebody. The journalists in the class started writing snide comments about PHIL-375 in their bi-weekly publication. There was a high level of distrust and repeated allegations of racism, homophobia, and classism. Students would come to my office and cry because they felt they had been misunderstood in class. Some students started staying away from class because they couldn't stand the accusations and recriminations.

We continued to plough our way through the readings,[4] but with none of the sense of joyful discovery I'd watched in my earlier class. By the end of the fall term I was convinced I'd chosen the wrong profession. I felt sick every time I went to class; I dreaded what new crisis might be generated.

Over the December break I knew I'd have to make some changes or I wouldn't survive the rest of the year, and I feared there would be serious problems among some of my students. Once again my students were pushing me to make changes, but this time they did not show me what changes to make.

I decided that it had not been sufficient merely to tell the students, at the beginning of the year, that mutual respect was necessary; there were some minimal conditions of respect and communication that had to be established, in practice, within the classroom. I also decided that the atmosphere had to be lightened up. We were discussing difficult and disheartening material about the forms and manifestations of oppression, but I didn't want the class to continue to be sunk in discouragement and alienation.

I decided that we would have to recognize and admit that many of us were not going to be "comfortable" in this class. When the new term started in January, I suggested

---

4 These now included Frye 1983; hooks 1988; Garry and Pearsall 1989; and Bartky 1990.

that we continue to work for conditions of safety in the class, so that everyone would be treated with respect and listened to with interest, but that safety was not the same as comfort. I tried to stress the idea of reaching out across apparent "barriers" to win each other as allies.

At the beginning of each class I introduced go-rounds.[5] My aim was to have every student speak, so that some of the shyest and most intimidated would no longer be silent. Another aim was to help students get to know each other as something more than political symbols, and to introduce a positive note at the beginning of the class before we dove into the issues. Sometimes I asked everyone briefly to describe something that was "new and good" in their lives. Sometimes I asked them to relate something they were looking forward to, or something they were proud of. At other times I asked a question oriented directly to the content of the work in the course. The question needed to be flexible enough to enable each person to speak and raise issues of concern to her/him—for example, "Describe something that's interesting/ problematic/controversial about the topic or reading for today." The result of answering these questions was that every member of the class was enabled to establish a pattern of speaking out, and we started to get some sense

---

5 "Go-rounds" are also useful at other times in the class—for example, when people are falling silent, when only a few are dominating discussion, or when there is a need to inject new ideas into the conversation. At the end of a meeting, a "go-round" can be used to complete the class on a positive note ("Describe something you're looking forward to"), or to offer closure on the day's discussion ("Describe something you changed your mind about during the discussion." "What is one issue on which your views were confirmed?" "What is one question from today's discussion that still puzzles you?").

of the members of the class as full human beings, with lives outside of academia and beyond politics.

The other change I introduced into the class was a stronger emphasis on listening skills, derived from what I'd learned in Re-Evaluation Counseling. As I pointed out in Chapter 3, much philosophical training—and indeed, academic training in general—involves learning to attack, to be aggressive, to look for flaws and fallacies in reasoning (Moulton 1989). These students, most of whom were used to competing for air space both in other classes and in political meetings, often found it difficult to adopt the role of listener. So, for some discussion topics I invited the students to pair up with another member of the class whom they did not yet know well or with whom they had significant disagreements. I emphasized that for half the time each student would talk and for half, each student would listen. I said that the listener should not interrupt, not launch into a discussion of her own views, not argue, not make "helpful" comments, not prompt in any fashion, but simply listen in a relaxed, attentive, interested way, maintaining eye contact wherever possible. The listening dyad is designed to help each person to "think out loud" with a respectful, interested listener. The talker is encouraged just to enjoy the opportunity to follow his/her thought, without regard for having to defend him/herself against another person's criticisms. I added that if the speaker ran out of things to say while "her/his time" was still running, the listener should just wait in respectful, expectant silence.[6]

---

6 Topics and questions for the dyads need not require students to "bare their souls." They can simply use students' experience by drawing upon events, activities, and practices they have

The tale of my 1991-92 class does not have a particularly happy ending. I can't say that introducing deliberate
measures to promote respect and communication transformed the group. Invoking students' experiences outside
politics and academia did not obviate all of the anger.
But it did enable us to keep talking to each other, though
the process remained painful. And it enabled all of us,
and especially me, to get to the end of the year without
giving up in despair.

What I Learned

As my tale of two classes suggests, I made changes in my
teaching because I was pushed, in different ways, by my
students. My motivation was intellectual, to enable students to understand and evaluate the material, not just
passively receive it; political, to make my classes more
relevant to the social issues we were considering; psychological, to render the classroom a more pleasant place to
be; and moral, to establish the minimum conditions of
respect and trust to enable communication to take place.
And because the classes became more interesting, more
productive, and more positive, making these changes was
in my own self-interest as an instructor and scholar.

The challenges I faced in these two classes helped me
to understand some general principles about teaching
and learning, principles that continue to guide my behaviour in the classroom. As the multiple moral of my story,
I list them here.

witnessed. The questions can be used to encourage students to
apply concepts covered in the course, or to test claims made in
the readings.

1. To some extent, method is content: that is, part of what is being learned is conveyed by the way it is taught. Philosophy is not a subject to be passively absorbed but a way of thinking, speaking, and writing that can be actively practised. I attempt to model the cognitive skills that I'd like my students to acquire and use: the skills of listening, understanding, assessing, arguing, and creating alternatives. Then I use deliberate strategies to encourage students to do likewise. There is, of course, an ominous side to this pedagogy: the students as a mere "reproduction" of the teacher, or more generally, as the "impersonation of an educated person, taking on and reproducing the style and tastes of a [socio-economic] class" (Gallop 1995, 4). However, the virtue of philosophy at its best is that it is a reflexive process, inviting and supporting self-criticism as well as criticism of the models that, for pedagogical and intellectual purposes, are—however briefly—emulated.

2. I want the classroom to be an example of a place where difficult issues can be dealt with intensively, rigorously, but also respectfully. My goal is to create an environment where students feel reasonably safe and encouraged to examine the issues. But I distinguish between safety and comfort: while I want them to feel safe to speak out, I do not promise that they will always feel comfortable. They may hear views that make them uncomfortable: this is often where learning begins.

3. The university class is a social organism that grows and develops over time. It's possible, unfortunately, to hinder that growth, but it's also possible to foster it. Every class has a different personality. I want to enable

that personality to develop in a way that promotes mutual respect and learning. I want the class to become an intellectually supportive community. Although, as Susan Miller comments, "the students in a class … embody a class, a collective whose interests are not always mine" (Miller 1995, 164), I seek to find a way for the class's interests to be expressed and realized that is consistent with the academy's intellectual mission and my own moral purposes.

4. As a feminist, I'm committed to the truth of the basic feminist idea, "The personal is political." I also believe that the personal is educational, that is, that part of what we can learn in philosophy comes from using our own experiences as a means of applying concepts, testing observations, and understanding viewpoints. I explore this theme further in Chapter 8.

5. It is important for everyone to participate in each class, as much as possible. I tell students from the beginning that my goal is for everyone to contribute. To help achieve that goal, I emphasize listening. The listening techniques I use are different from debating or discussing; they are designed to foster conversations and to help each person to "think out loud" with a respectful, interested listener, without having to engage in the usual academic defence tactics.

6. I try to encourage innovation: the introduction of alternative ways of doing and learning philosophy, by means of dialogues, go-rounds, role-playing, group discussions, and writing interludes. I also put a strong emphasis on the development of writing skills, giving

students the opportunity to produce outlines and drafts of work in progress, for which I offer comments and suggestions.

7. Students learn a lot about what's important from each other, not just from me, and not only through their interactions in the classroom. Learning will go on outside the classroom, especially if people build the relationships that will enable them to continue talking. In the long run I want to encourage students to become independent learners who are not reliant on me either for the motivation or the capacity to continue philosophizing long after the course is over.

What is common to—and at least partially constitutive of—the various classes I have taught is the constant fact of our mutual disappearance from each other: after a term or a year each class, along with its diverse members, disappears from my professional life, while I, as instructor, disappear from theirs. We are only a chapter in each other's lives; at best we learn enough from each other to enable us to go on to the next chapter. And if we are sufficiently insightful (as I was certainly not, at least at first) we recognize that while each class may seem to be "just another course" from the perspective of both student and teacher, each experience of the enduring pedagogical relationship is unique and offers its own distinctive challenges.

CHAPTER 5

"Nowhere At Home"

> [W]hat does it mean to ascend [from the working class] to the *academy*? Because the interests of the two classes are inimical and the cultural styles antagonistic, the mobile person is often torn between competing loyalties and adrift with respect to his or her sense of membership in class culture. It is the sense of being nowhere at home. (Ryan and Sackrey 1984, 119, their emphasis)

Prologue

In 1989 I was invited to a birthday party in the neighbourhood where I grew up in the 1950s and 1960s. The party was for a friend from my high school years—a friend who never went to university and never left the working-class suburb of Toronto where I once lived. At that party, surrounded by people still living where their parents had lived, still doing the sorts of jobs their parents did, I felt like a frivolous tropical goldfish in a small pond full of sensible hard-working minnows. To the other party-goers I was both ostentatiously visible yet almost incomprehensible. When I mentioned to my friend that I would soon be flying to Edmonton to read a paper, she replied pertly, "Can't they read it themselves?"

But for me the most revealing event in the evening occurred very late, after midnight, when all of us had danced a lot, eaten a lot, and drunk a lot, just as we used to twenty years earlier. A large, florid-faced, sweating man, who in high school had been a dedicated football player, drew me out into a hallway, because, he said, he wanted to ask me an important question. I waited for what I anticipated would be a sexually aggressive or mocking comment. Instead he surprised me by saying, in a tone scarcely above a whisper, "How did you get out?"

In an article entitled "The Structure of Proletarian Unfreedom,"[1] philosopher G.A. Cohen undertakes to show that, in an important sense, workers are *forced* to sell their labour-power. He argues that while a small minority of proletarians are individually free to escape their class position by rising into the petty bourgeois, "each is free only on condition that the others do not exercise their similarly conditional freedom"; that is, proletarians may be individually free but they are collectively unfree (Cohen 1986, 244). He uses a disturbing image to bring his thesis to life:

> Ten people are placed in a room the only exit from which is a huge and heavy locked door. At various distances from each lies a single heavy key. Whoever picks up this key—and each is physically able, with varying degrees of effort, to do so—and takes it to the door will find, after considerable self-application, a way to open the door and leave the room. But if he does so he alone will be able to leave it. Photoelectric devices installed by a jailer ensure that it will open only just enough to permit one exit. Then it will close, and no one inside the room will be able to open it again. (Cohen 1986, 242)

---

1 I am grateful to my working-class colleague Henry Laycock for drawing this paper to my attention.

The poignancy of the situation that Cohen describes lies partly in the fact that each person's exercise of freedom by exiting from the working class is a threat to the others' freedom to leave. But what strikes me most forcibly about Cohen's image is his assumption that the people in the room will know that they are locked in, will believe in a world outside the room, will recognize the key as the means of escape, and will even attempt to seize it. For although workers in this culture may recognize that some persons do not sell their labour power to survive, more than this recognition is required to identify their own position and see the possibility of escape—especially the kind of collective escape that would constitute the end of class society. The power of the class system in North America persists, in part, because of its simultaneous invisibility and apparent naturalness. Hence, to me, the pathos of the ex-football player's question was that, unlike most of the other party-goers, he believed that there is something to escape from, that there is something to escape to, that escape is possible, and that escape is worthwhile. For, unlike the ex-football player, many working-class people don't know that they are locked in a room, or that there is anywhere else to go. The key is imperceptible, or appears valueless, or is too heavy. And the few who escape from the room soon forget where they have come from.

I, however, am among those who, in the words of Carie Winslow, "spend their lives trying to get out of neighborhoods they grew up in or occupations they were slotted for by grade 4" (Winslow 1991-92, 50).[2] At the age

---

2 I am grateful to Dawn Tunnicliffe for drawing my attention to the Winter 1991-92 issue of *Sinister Wisdom*, in which several articles on class issues quoted in this chapter appear.

of twelve I decided that education would be my way of avoiding a future as a waitress, factory worker, or clerk-typist. As a teenager I was powerfully affected by a song called "We Gotta Get Out of This Place." If education was the ticket out, I was determined to get as far as I possibly could. Three degrees later, I still have not left academia, convinced as I am that education remains my only protection from what would otherwise be a working-class destiny.

Of course, I haven't entirely escaped the working class. I have not escaped in Cohen's sense, for I still sell my labour-power. I am compelled to do so, for, despite Cohen's theoretical freedom to advance into the petty bourgeois, I have no sources of independent wealth and neither the talent nor the resources for becoming an entrepreneur. Indeed, the loss of my partner's job only served to emphasize the total dependency of our family of two adults and two children on my wage. So I remain working class insofar as I am, as the working-class writer Dan Nickerson defines it, "dependent on a wage drawn from the fruits of [my] own labor" (Nickerson 1991, 53).

Moreover, I am still working class in another sense defined by Nickerson: I still "identify with working-class culture—the values and lifestyles of the generally non-college-educated, wage-earning people" (Nickerson 1991, 57). While working-class culture is not, by any means, uniform and monolithic, it socializes its participants, as my later discussion will show, to see the world with different beliefs, hopes, and expectations from those held by middle-class people. Despite my lengthening sojourn in academia, the experiences and assumptions of the working-class kid from Toronto still animate my life.

Nevertheless, my life represents my parents' vision of escape, for I have moved from the class of "people who are engaged in the direct production of goods or services and not generally paid for their thinking but for their production" (Nickerson 1991, 57) into the middle class, which Nickerson defines as "that group of workers who do not work in the direct delivery of goods and services but who work in support of the direct production of goods and services in their roles as organizers, teachers, managers, and consultants" (Nickerson 1991, 54). And, insofar as I live, as an academic, more comfortably, more freely, and less precariously than my parents did, I have in this way at least escaped from my working-class background.

The Phenomenology of a Working-Class Academic

In what follows I hope to demonstrate both the necessity and the fruitfulness for academics, particularly academics with working-class origins, of a form of feminist consciousness-raising with respect to class. It can teach us both about the ambiguities of escaping from the working-class and about the ways in which academia contributes to the difficulty of escape.

I want to explore what I call the "phenomenology" of a working-class academic's consciousness. My inspiration is, in part, philosopher Sandra Lee Bartky's investigation, in her landmark paper, "Toward a Phenomenology of Feminist Consciousness" (Bartky, 1990), of the phenomenology of gender and the "profound personal transformation" of becoming a feminist. First published in 1976, Bartky's discussion is still relevant today. But whereas her work delineates her growing awareness of the social category of "woman," I wish to delineate some aspects of my growing awareness of the social category of "academic from a working-class background."

Working-class academics are ironically described by Jake Ryan and Charles Sackrey as "strangers in para-dise,"[3] in their eponymous book (Ryan and Sackrey 1984). The autobiographical stories they present are fascinating but somewhat foreign to my experience, primarily because almost all of their story-tellers are male, most entered university employment during the 1950s and 1960s, and many came to academia after serving in the United States military. I, however, write as a Canadian woman who was an undergraduate in the late 1960s and has been employed in academia—first in a junior college, then in a university—since the mid-1970s.

This discussion is also inspired by my fairly recent recognition that the phenomena associated with sexism are not adequate to fully account for my discomfort with-in the academic community. For I occupy a minority sta-tus not only by virtue of my sex but by virtue of my class origins, and the analysis by some feminist scholars of the situation of women in academia—an analysis that usual-ly emphasizes gender, race, and, less frequently, sexual orientation—seems inadequate to account for both the reality and my perception of my situation as an outsider.

In much of the women's studies literature before the 1990s, what might be called "middle-class solipsism" pre-vailed; that is, the assumption that membership in the

---

3 I am grateful to Chuck Barone, who in 1988 led a support group for academics from working-class backgrounds which I was fortunate to join, and who half-ironically encouraged us to consider seeing ourselves as "strangers in paradise."

middle class is the norm and goes without saying, whereas working-class membership is deviant enough to have
to be signalled by an explicit allusion. General references
to class were—and sometimes still are—often curiously
empty of that experiential core that animates discussions
of gender and race. "… and class" became the tail-end of
a litany that included all the usual dimensions of oppression and "marginalization," yet the inclusion of class
remained theoretical, with insufficient basis in an awareness of the difference that class location makes to how we
live. But as Elliott, a working-class lesbian writer, points
out, "class isn't about theory. Class is about survival,
about which of us will and won't make it" (Elliott 1991-
92, 39).

Possibly the experiences of working-class attachment
and membership received less attention than experiences
related to gender, race, and sexual orientation because
while (apparently) one's sex, race, and sexual orientation
remain more or less intact upon entry into academia,
working-class people seem to leave their class behind in
order to succeed in the university. So class appears to be
a superficial characteristic, perhaps a matter of the
clothes we choose to wear or the foods we happen to like,
rather than what it is: a status that can be constitutive of
one's sense of oneself, one's place in the world, and one's
hopes and prospects.

I have noticed that my attempts to discuss my working-class origins and their current significance within the
university are often received with a certain discomfort
best represented by the response, "Why do you have to
keep talking about it?" This is a response activists have
seen before—with respect to women's issues, gay/
lesbian/bisexual issues, and race issues. It is a sign that

something important is being discussed, something that makes people self-conscious, perhaps, about their current privileges. In a written dialogue with bell hooks on race and class, Mary Childers suggests,

> Many privileged women are made uncomfortable by stories of the abuse rather than the help doled out [to working-class children] by middle-class teachers, preachers, social workers, store owners, classmates, etc. They don't want to realize that their class has been a sphere of trauma for others or to remember the ways in which they participated in mocking poor kids in the second grade. (Childers and hooks 1990, 72)

In my university department, the persons with whom I seem to have most in common and who have consistently acted as my allies over the past decade are the secretaries with whom I share a similar class background. At the same time, I experience a recurrent and shameful envy of my middle-class students, especially the well-groomed, knowledgeable, confident young middle-class women who are able to take for granted their right to be at the university and their ability to function well there. I also sense a certain distance from certain of my middle-class female colleagues. For example, I felt resentment (though I did not express it) toward a feminist academic who remarked, at a social gathering, that she and her husband were going to be "poor" for a year while they went to Oxford on sabbatical, living on one salary, and renting out their gorgeous house back home. I was reminded of writer Caryatis Cardea's comment to middle-class women:

Poverty is not-having-money due to conditions beyond one's control. To choose to be relatively moneyless within an essentially self-controlled life is simply not poverty. You'll just have to come up with another term (or, preferably, knock it off!) and disabuse yourselves of the notion that your lives in any way resemble the lives of poor people. (Cardea 1991-92, 108)

I suggest that discussions of class should take root from the theorized experience of our class origins; we need to develop a phenomenology of class.[4] In what remains of this chapter my intent is to explore some aspects of my consciousness, as a working-class academic, of self and of social reality (Bartky 1990, 12). This is no generalized class consciousness, although generalizations from it may be possible. It consists of a series of fairly specific internalized conflicts. As Ryan and Sackrey remark, "[T]o grow up working class, then to take on the full trappings of the life of the college professor, *internalizes the conflicts in the hierarchy of the class system within the individual, upwardly mobile person*" (Ryan and Sackrey 1984, 5, their emphasis).

To paraphrase Bartky, working-class consciousness is the consciousness of a being radically alienated from one's world and often divided against oneself (Bartky 1990, 21). Yet these conflicts can also be a source of insight and strength. As bell hooks remarks,

Contradictions are perceived as chaos and not orderly, not rational, everything doesn't follow. Coming out of

---

4 See Frost (1997) as well as Tokarczyk and Fay's excellent collection of papers by working-class women in academia (1993) for examples of this type of work.

academe, many of us want to present ourselves as just
that: orderly, rational. We also then must struggle for a
language that allows us to say: we have contradictions
and those contradictions do not necessarily make us
quote 'bad people' or politically unsound people.
(Childers and hooks 1990, 70)

Indeed, they may teach us something important about
both the place we've come from and the place we're in
now.

Conflicts

1) The contrast between class identity and gender identity is informative. Unlike class identity, one's gender
identity is usually quite visible; in fact, it is socially
expected and required that each of us announce our gender identity, both continuously and ostentatiously (Frye
1983b). As a result of feminists' attention to this performance of gender (e.g., Butler 1990) there is a growing
awareness in the academy of both the dimensions of gender construction and its oppressive consequences. By
contrast, one's class identity is, and is expected to be,
much less obvious, especially at the university, where
wealthy students dress in ragged jeans, and poorer students inconspicuously work twenty or thirty hours a
week, "part time," in order to be able to afford the same
social life funded, in the rich kids' case, by daddy. It is
hard for working-class people—whether students or
faculty—to recognize the difference that class makes;
after all, we're all here at university, aren't we? In fact, I
had been teaching for thirteen years before I explicitly

identified my origins as working class. Whereas university women—faculty, staff, and students—are more and more feeling and expressing solidarity around issues of sexism, there is little discernible sense of cooperation or communality among those from a working-class background. There is little awareness of the dimensions of class construction and its oppressive consequences.

At the same time, and apparently paradoxically, despite the relative difficulty of detecting and appreciating people's class identities, I have succeeded in internalizing considerable contempt for my own class origins. Regrettably, like many others, I have naively and unwittingly bought into the oppressive connotations of escape: that partially escaping my working-class origins somehow makes them not important; or that anyone can leave, if they just work hard enough; or even that my working-class roots weren't real, never existed. Like self-described "working-class intellectual" Martha Courtot,

> In order to succeed in the world I [have had] to deny my deep root system and to become something different, a social construct of an upwardly-mobile working person who would succeed or fail depending on how much of myself I could remove, forget, leave behind. (Courtot 1991-92, 89)

The difficulty of recognizing one's working-class origins and their significance is a result of the operation of internalized oppression. While G.A. Cohen does not explicitly acknowledge the importance of internalized oppression, he allows for the possibility for it when he distinguishes in his paper between the freedom to do something and the capacity to do it (Cohen 1986, 254-5):

"if one lacks the capacity to do A as a result of the action of others, then one is not only incapable of doing A but also unfree to do it." The lack of capacity to recognize one's working-class origins is, in part, the result of internalized limitations on freedom—limitations created by a political system that encourages acquiescence and hopelessness, a mass culture that values fulfilment through material acquisition, and a primary and secondary education system that discourages children both from dreaming and from criticizing.

My first conflict, then, is between, on the one hand, the invisibility of class and the consequent mystification of my class identity, and on the other hand, the internalization of disdain for my working-class origins and the desire to transcend them.

2) What has recently been dubbed the "imposter syndrome" is not just a phenomenon of gender; class refugees are also subject to it. Students from working-class backgrounds have told me that one of their biggest challenges at the university is to "pass" as middle class; that is, to conceal their stigmatized class origins.

Like Carie Winslow, "I still have a high investment in not being found out. My mom taught me that it was important to hide being poor" (Winslow 1991-92, 49). I have to cope with feeling both intelligent and stupid at once: intelligent enough to have succeeded, in the ex-football player's words, in "getting out," but not bright enough to become just "one of the boys" in the university environment. The legacy of a working-class upbringing is the shame of being a misfit, the feeling of not being good enough or smart enough to succeed in middle-class academia: at any moment, someone may find out that I am not really the scholar and intellectual I have tried so hard to be.[5] It is not surprising that, after being a non-stop talker all through primary and secondary school, on my working-class home turf, I became completely silent at university and only slowly, painfully, regained my voice when I saw that speaking out was part of the price of success. And so my second conflict is between the sense of false superiority/uniqueness at having been "smart" enough to escape from the working class into academia and the feeling of being a scholastic fraud, a working-class bull in the university china shop.

Growing up in working-class Toronto, I had, unlike my middle-class colleagues, little or no access to foreign travel, classical and contemporary art, dance, and theatre, fine cuisine, elegant clothes, middle-class manners, and influential people. Before I went to university, no one in my family had ever written a term paper or sat in a lecture hall, and no one could explain to me how to communicate with professors (none of us had ever met a professor), how to dig out obscure information in the library, which extra-curricular activities would be useful, what magazines and journals to read, how to handle myself at social events, or where to find a summer job that would complement my studies rather than just exhausting me (we didn't have the right "connections"). Like the philosopher Robert Nozick, I am an "immigrant to the realm of thought" (Nozick 1981, viii). As a result, I never felt that I knew the academic rules—especially the unwritten ones—well enough to participate as an equal with my supposed peers. I had to learn, slowly and painfully, to "pass" as middle class.

---

5 I discuss other manifestations and implications of the feeling of fraudulence in Chapter 6.

3) Because we were not exposed to and governed by the same rules as children of the middle class, working-class kids may not be "nice." As writer Tammis Coffin notes, people from working-class origins often are potential "trouble-makers" (Coffin 1992, 48), insofar as we have less commitment to the middle-class rules, practices, and niceties that we never entirely learned or understood. Less burdened by notions of what is "proper" in social situations, we may be more "direct and able to get to the point" (Coffin 1992, 47) and more expressive of our feelings (not all of which are positive). As Childers and hooks observe, this openness can be threatening to middle-class people (Childers and hooks 1990, 70-71). Often, we have seen more of the gritty, hard-working, dangerous side of life than have our colleagues who have spent their lives in the middle class.

In discussing her experience as a woman of colour in a predominantly white world, the philosopher Maria Lugones suggests that "the outsider has necessarily acquired flexibility in shifting from the mainstream construction of life where she is constructed as an outsider to other constructions of life where she is more or less 'at home'" (Lugones 1989, 275). Similarly, for the ambitious working-class person the capacity for what Lugones calls "world-traveling," that is, the ability to shift from the "dominant culture's description and construction of life" to a "nondominant" or "idiosyncratic" construction (Lugones 1989, 281, 282), becomes a necessary skill.[6] And, as Lugones suggests, world-travelling can be a source both of insight and of ambivalence; it can result in being "nowhere at home."

6 See Chapter 7 for a discussion of another form of "world"-travelling.

When I was sixteen a high school teacher chastised me for using what he called "bad grammar." That same year a friend was amazed when I used the word "inebriated" to describe a drunk. But at that age I already understood (though I could not have explicitly stated) that I had to speak two languages: the vernacular of working-class adolescents and adults, complete with slang, neologisms, and linguistic constructions that did not follow the grammar textbook, and the jargon of (semi-)educated middle-class adults, with both its more sophisticated vocabulary and its greater constraints on acceptable speech. We have different characteristics within different worlds, says Lugones (Lugones 1989, 281). As an adolescent, I was bilingual, but I sometimes failed to use the language relevant to each world; I had to avoid displaying my bilingualism inappropriately within each of the worlds I had to inhabit. This difficulty persists: within academia, I must remember and deliberately choose to tone down my expressiveness and exuberance, be sure I know how to pronounce words that I have learned only through reading, and curb my tendency to use a relaxed, colloquial speaking style. On the other hand, among those from my own background, I have been greeted with incomprehension, laughter, and even contempt when I accidentally used a word such as "demographics" in ordinary conversation.

Even while acknowledging the strengths of my working-class background, it is important for me not to romanticize its impoverishments—of understanding, education, opportunity, and thought. There is a certain moral error in speaking of one's working-class upbringing "as a kind of accomplishment" (Jeremy Seabrook, quoted in Steedman 1987, 15). It is the error of inappropriately applying what Frye calls "the arrogant eye" to my own background. The arrogant eye "organize[s] everything seen with reference to [itself] and [its] own interests" (Frye 1983a, 67). For me the working class was something to survive, overcome, and escape from; but for my parents it represented the best they could provide while raising their children, and for many of my childhood friends it remains the only life they know.

And so the third conflict is between feeling that speaking out about the reality of my working-class roots is a disloyal, even pretentious, appropriation of my family's struggles and also believing that my origins have conferred special strengths, including the determination to persist in work for which my background never prepared me.

4) Despite my sensation of being an outsider, a displaced person in academia, I am also dogged, especially in recessionary times, by the feeling that I should be grateful to have a job at all, especially one that *looks* so much easier than anything my parents and grandparents had to do, in terms of pay, self-determination, and comfort. As Ryan and Sackrey express it,

> Career consciousness and its careful nurturance ... is [*sic*] a skill much more easily learned in a middle or upper class family.... Alternatively, *having* a job and *keeping* it, is [*sic*] more a working class perspective on the world of work. (Ryan and Sackrey 1984, 90, their emphasis)

One of their contributors writes, "Middle class folk expect to have rewarding careers.... Other folks have jobs. And if they're lucky, the jobs aren't too bad. Compared with the rest of my family, I'm lucky" (Ryan and Sackrey 1984, 293). And writer Marilyn Murphy suggests,

> Most upwardly mobile working and poverty class women feel like frauds in our middle-class jobs. The jobs are not *really* work to us. We feel guilty about the money we make, so much more than our parents made for standing on their feet all day and taking abuse. (Murphy 1991, 39)

As a result, as Murphy points out, upwardly-mobile working-class women may over-work and take abuse on the job—perhaps because it is harder for us to recognize when the job is exploitive. After all, the work is clean, reasonably quiet, not obviously physically dangerous. How can subtle harassment, a workload of 150 students and nine committees, and the expectation of constant availability from students and faculty alike be considered to be bad working conditions? In general, while I am highly critical of academia in general and my own institution in particular, I also feel inordinately thankful for the things it gives me: a library full of books, an office all to myself, interesting students, and legitimation for thinking and writing.

And so my fourth conflict is between, on the one hand, bemusement at the fact that I can get paid for activities that seem not to be "real work" but "mere" reading, writing, and speaking, and, on the other hand, pride in and gratitude for my job: it is no mere dilettantism, but my very life.

Epilogue

This newly-developing consciousness of myself as an academic from the working class has had effects on my teaching, my research, and my perception of the university. I shall mention just one example.

In an attempt to compensate for the declining government funding of post-secondary education, significant increases in tuition fees have been instituted during the 1990s at my institution (as at most others in Canada). In some years recently, the student government, as well as much of the student body, has not always been concerned about these changes. A substantial number of our undergraduate students, many of whom come from comfortable middle-class or wealthy families, have supported proposals for increased fees, which they believe will improve learning conditions that have deteriorated as a result of government under-funding. They also think that less wealthy kids will not be unduly burdened because of the provision of increased scholarships and bursaries.

I know, however, that no matter how much financial aid is improved, high tuition fees discriminate against working-class students and contribute to the preservation of class distinctions in academia; they make escape more difficult. I chose my undergraduate institution entirely on the basis of financial considerations: it was nearby enough to enable me to continue to live at home and thus not incur the expenses of independent living, and it offered me full funding for tuition and books, unlike the other, newer university in town, whose programs I preferred, but which could offer me only a partial scholarship. Back where I come from, higher tuition fees are likely to be perceived by prospective students as a real obstacle. The public image of the expensive education will prevail over any added information about financial assistance. In my old neighbourhood people are reluctant to take big financial risks: they won't bet on a mysterious system that might or might not give them money to compensate for its high costs. Students from working-class families will not assume that they will be the ones to receive the extra funds; after all, their families don't have a history of luck with money. With good reason, they also fear the prospect of finishing university with a debt the size of a home mortgage. If they decide they need more education after high school, they are more likely to choose a less expensive community college. And so, as a result of reasoning such as this, I find myself more radical than some of my students: while some of them contemplate and even vote for increased tuition fees, I hold a view many regard as archaic: I support a policy of zero tuition.

For working-class kids, higher education is a curious-ly ambiguous phenomenon. Ironically, it is both a way out of some working-class limitations, yet it also con-tributes to making that escape difficult. In other words, to use Cohen's terms, the university is a route to individ-ual freedom even while it helps to preserve collective unfreedom. As Ryan and Sackrey emphasize, academics

> contribute, consciously or not, to the reproduction of the system itself which keeps cultural and class relationships more or less in order.... [The academy] does much to support the meritocratic ideology which claims entitlement to privilege and reward those capable of high levels of achievement and the hindmost

for the most ordinary plodder. (Ryan and Sackrey 1984, 108, 109)

The presence in the university of faculty from the working class appears to confirm the "myth of upward mobility"—the idea that our origins have no impact on our chances of success. We must buy into academia in order to get out of the working class, but in doing so we also buy into the denigration of our background and the preservation of class inequities. In the end, it seems, the price of successful escape is to be intellectually and socially "nowhere at home."

CHAPTER 6

Feeling Fraudulent

"The kind of classroom situation one creates is the acid test of what it is one really stands for.... What we do in the classroom is our politics," says literary theorist Jane Tompkins (1991, 26, 27).

And, I would add, what we do in the classroom is also our ethics.

Surprisingly, philosophy professors seldom talk or write about the ethics of university teaching—unless driven to it, *in extremis*, by ethical crises, such as sexual or racial harassment, plagiarism, or unfairness to students. While there exist academic studies of the inculcation of ethical standards in professional programmes (Ozar 1993), empirical investigations of graduate students' exposure to academic misconduct (Anderson, Louis, and Earle 1994), vignettes of problems researchers could have with respect to graduate student researchers and assistants (Medical Research Council 1994), lists of possible ethical problems in teaching (Svinicki 1994), and discussions of the teaching of values (Collins 1983), the ethical world of university teaching includes much more. Some examples are "how instructors decide whom to call on, how they balance out individual and group needs, how they deal with misplaced or incorrect comments, and how they keep their own views from stifling wide-ranging classroom debates" (David A. Garvin 1991, 288). As Garvin remarks, "Selecting and assigning readings, presenting ideas, grading and evaluating students—the basic stuff of classroom life—involve decisions of unexpected ethical import" (1991, 287).

In this chapter I am interested in exploring some ethical dimensions of university teaching. I begin at an unlikely location: the feeling of fraudulence. Tracing the origins of this feeling reveals some moral quandaries in the situation of university instructors, especially feminist instructors. I suggest some possible causes for feeling fraudulent, attempt to assess its significance, and then sketch some ways of revisioning, if not resolving, the moral quandaries that the feeling of fraudulence reveals.

Feeling Fraudulent

In Mary McCarthy's novel, *The Groves of Academe*, one of the characters, Howard Furness, believes that the entire academic world is divided into three groups. He calls these groups the "admitted frauds, [the] hypocritical frauds, [and the] unconscious frauds." "[T]his fraudulence," says McCarthy, "in fact, to [Howard's] glazed-pottery-blue eye, constituted the human" (McCarthy 1951, 100).

As an academic I often feel that I should align myself with the first category, the admitted frauds. The term captures a deep uneasiness at the heart of my experience as an academic. I even fantasize about opening a special chapter of Frauds Anonymous for university instructors:

"I am Professor X and I am a fraud." For when I teach, I suffer from the imposter syndrome.

The imposter syndrome is, in my experience, primarily a feeling that I cannot live up to the external image of myself. It is not a matter of deliberate insincerity or dishonesty. Rather, I have a fear that I am not what I am supposed to be—that is, an academic expert. The university environment and its components—students, administration, other faculty members—impose standards I fear I am not able to meet. Survival in the academy requires that I nonetheless attempt to meet them. There is a disjunction between who I am expected to be, on the one hand, and on the other, what I think I actually can do. Somehow I have managed to deceive students, colleagues, and administrators about my competence—but any day now I may be exposed as a person who does not really know what she is doing.

Both informal conversations and formal research suggest that I am not alone in feeling fraudulent. Christopher Clark says, "We [teachers] want to look good all of the time. Asking for help makes us feel vulnerable—vulnerable to being discovered as imposters who don't know as much as we pretend to know" (Clark 1992, 82). And Tompkins remarks,

> Each person comes into a professional situation dragging along behind her a long bag full of desires, fears, expectations, needs, resentments—the list goes on. But the main component is fear.... *Fear of being shown up for what you are: a fraud*, stupid, ignorant, a clod, a dolt, a sap, a weakling, someone who can't cut the mustard. (Tompkins 1991, 25, my emphasis)

SOME SOURCES OF
FEELINGS OF FRAUDULENCE

What might be the causes of this feeling of fraudulence?

One possibility is that I really am a fraud: that during a history of more than thirty years in academia I have succeeded in deluding my own teachers, my colleagues, university administrators, and generations of students into believing, falsely, that I am competent.

However, not surprisingly, I want to give all those who have sat in judgment on me the benefit of the doubt. I have been hired, published, and promoted over the years; no one has accused me of being incompetent. Giving myself, too, the benefit of the doubt, I shall assume for the purposes of this investigation that I am not an imposter, despite my feelings to the contrary.

Instead, I want to suggest that there may be two general explanations for feelings of fraudulence: first, the intellectual constraints of our situation as instructors, and second, the nature of teaching as a performance. In addition, feminist academics may be particularly susceptible to feelings of fraudulence. There are two reasons: first, what I call the dilemma of audience, and second, our socially-imposed gender roles, exacerbated by ageism. In what follows I shall briefly explore the two general explanations and then discuss the situation of feminist academics.

THE INTELLECTUAL DEMANDS OF
OUR SITUATION AS INSTRUCTORS

Steven Cahn, author of one of the few book-length investigations of the ethics of university teaching, says (rather severely),

Instructors are obligated to guide the learning process. They are expected to know which material is to be studied and in what order it is best presented. They should be expected to know how individuals can proceed most productively. They should be expected to know what constitutes progress and the extent to which each student has achieved it. (Cahn 1986, 8)

And in her discussion of ethics in college teaching, Marilla Svinicki lists as an ethically dubious practice the teaching of material that one has "not yet fully mastered" (Svinicki 1994, 271).

But if Cahn's requirements are appropriate, and if teaching material one has not yet fully mastered is ethically dubious, then I, as an instructor of philosophy, am engaging in ethically dubious practices virtually every term. I am often undecided about what order in which to teach the topics in my courses. I am sometimes unclear about how to help students proceed "productively." And I frequently teach material I have "not yet fully mastered."

Uncertainty is the existential condition of scholars: Our own information, particularly as we have assembled it into understanding and interpretation, is inevitably partial. If we are intellectually alive, we acknowledge that fact each time we read an article that casts new light on a subject we thought we knew well. But it is not enough to be honest with ourselves in private; we must also find a way to be honest publicly, in the classroom, and that is terribly risky. It is a gesture of limitation, an admission of how far short of godlike

we are, and it is uncomfortable taking risks in front of a
room full of relative strangers. (Hildebidle 1991, 270)

What one of my own professors quaintly called "the
frontiers of knowledge" are not what they were twenty or
even ten years ago, nor what many of us were trained for.
For example, although I teach and research in feminist
philosophy, I had no training in that field. It didn't exist
when I was a student. Now, as I get older, as the material in my chosen fields of specialization becomes huge and
unwieldy, as my awareness of my own ignorance grows,
and as I lose the confidence I had two decades ago that I
had "solved" certain philosophical problems, the goal of
"mastering" material recedes ever farther from reach.

Epistemological questions also burden me: it is not
clear by what criteria I could be said to have mastered my
areas of competence or how I would be able to know that
I have. Subjective feelings of certainty (long gone in my
case) are no good indication. Academic recognition—
through publications and invitations to lecture—seems
fleeting and subject to a kind of perverse and unpredictable scholarly fashion.

Thus, the intellectual conditions for scholarship and
instruction may contribute to feelings of fraudulence.

TEACHING AS PERFORMANCE

Teaching is a solitary activity; except on the rare occasions when we engage in team teaching, it's a solo performance.

My teaching involves performance in at least two different senses. First, I (must) give a performance as I
teach, warming up for my role as instructor, preparing to

present a public exhibition of my philosophical skills. Especially with large classes, I must be ready to entertain, to sustain the attention of an audience accustomed to the excitement and fast pace of television and video. And whatever the size of the class, I must pretend enthusiasm on days when I feel none, withhold impatience at times when I am infused with it, and suppress anxiety or fear when these are my dominant emotions.

Teaching is also a performance in a second way. If my feelings of fraudulence lead me to fear that I'm not really an academic, then I can only pretend to be one. If I am not an authentic teacher, then I merely play the teacher, pretend to be the teacher. I don the behaviours and language of a genuine scholar. To act is not really to be. If I am giving a performance when I teach, then, it seems, I am not really being myself.

If I can't feel genuine while teaching, it's not surprising that I feel like an imposter. As Tomkins suggests, "Fear is the driving force behind the performance model" (Tomkins 1991, 25), primarily the fear of being shown up for what you "really" are. The nature of teaching as performance contributes to my feelings of fraudulence.

THE DILEMMA OF AUDIENCE

As a feminist I frequently confront what I call the dilemma of audience. On the one hand, I wish to convey feminist ideas, concepts, claims, and theories to the various student audiences I encounter—introductory classes, large lecture groups, small seminars. If those audiences are unfamiliar with feminism, or even—as they sometimes are—hostile to feminism, I confront two unpalatable alternatives. I can present feminist work—my work—as it is, directly and honestly, with whatever radicalness and criticism of the status quo that it may have. If I do so, I run the serious risk of not being heard at all, of being misunderstood, or of inciting so much hostility and insecurity in my listeners that they are unable to comprehend my message or assess it in any fair way.

Alternatively, I can reach out to my student audience, try to meet its members "where they live," and speak in a manner and in terms they find acceptable. As Marianna Torgovnick points out, "[W]hen critics want to be read, and especially when they want to be read by a large audience, they have to court their readers" (Torgovnick, quoted in Young-Bruehl, 33). If I do "court" my audience, however, I run the serious risk of misrepresenting my own views, of watering them down, of making them soft enough, mainstream enough, unthreatening enough, that the audience will hear and will understand, may even agree—but it is no longer my own genuine views that they are accepting.

So the dilemma of audience gives me the choice of either alienating my audience or betraying myself—and sometimes both at once. In both cases, I fail to communicate what I really believe. No wonder I feel fraudulent.

SOCIALLY-IMPOSED GENDER ROLES AND AGEISM

My sense of fraudulence is also a complex product of expectations founded upon my sex and my age.

Academic expectations are gendered. "[W]ho we are, as we are positioned both institutionally and as bodies in the world, conditions the effect of what we say" (Ardis 1992, 168). Philosophy professor Ann Ardis discusses how her perceived physical being—female, short, young—compromises her authority in the classroom. Unlike Ardis, for me youth is no longer a handicap. But middle age brings its own socially-fostered handicaps.

Mary Wilson Carpenter names the combination of ageism and sexism in academia "Sexagism" [*sic*] (Carpenter 1996, 142). She argues that ageism not only affects women in general more than men, but because of cultural expectations associated with female sexuality and reproduction, it "impacts on *academic* women disproportionately in comparison to academic men" (Carpenter 1996, 143, her emphasis).

In my experience, sexagism allows students to see me as a mother—as their mother, as a symbolic mother, even as the parody of a mother. Susan Stanford Friedman remarks, "students may pressure any woman-teacher to fulfil the role of the all-forgiving, nurturing mother whose approval is unconditional" (Friedman 1985, 206). Certainly I experience pressures from students to exhibit stereotypical maternal behaviour: to be reassuring, supportive, nurturant; not to criticize or insist; to believe them no matter what they say.

But as Margaret Talbot points out,

> female professors aren't necessarily any nicer, more indulgent, more intuitively ethical, than their male counterparts. Just like the guys, they sometimes hand out bad grades, refuse to write letters of recommendation, pack reading lists with their own books, turn importuning freshmen away at their office doors. Only it's worse, because students, especially women, want more time and expect more comfort from female professors. (Talbot 1994, 29)

So I may also be seen through the lens of another maternal stereotype: the rejecting yet possessive and bossy hausfrau, who wants her academic offspring to go on doing things her way, who fails to recognize true innovation because of her devotion to the way things were.

The more I am perceived as a mother-stereotype, the more I am faced with the Catch-22 of either withdrawing from the role or attempting to play up to it. I have no desire to be the surrogate mother of my students. At the same time, the pressure to provide mothering is difficult to resist. Perhaps I *should* play the role of the good mother? Would it clearly differentiate my work from the problematic behaviours of some of my male colleagues? Would I be most effective in that function? How can I avoid being seen as the bad mother?

Not every woman scholar, I assume, is seen as a mother, or mother stereotype. Depending partly on their age, some others may be seen as little sisters, female confidantes, even sexual predators or prey. But in general, the expectations generated by standard female gender roles at various life stages contribute to feelings of fraudulence. For conformity to the stereotypes is not only difficult but self-compromising: we are both more and other than the women we are expected to be. Compliance with stereotypes means a loss of personal integrity, while failure to comply may render us almost unrecognizable.

A Contradiction at the Heart of Teaching

Although I reject the mother role that some students try to assign to me, my understanding of my feelings of fraudulence has been further enhanced by a concept derived from Sara Ruddick's discussion of mothering. Her analysis of a deep contradiction, within maternal practice, between the goals of growth and acceptability sheds light on a comparable problem in teaching practice, particularly feminist teaching. It helps to explain, though not dissolve, feelings of fraudulence.

According to Ruddick, maternal practice[1] is governed by three interests: the preservation, growth, and acceptability of the child (Ruddick 1989, 215). Whereas the interest of preservation requires the labour of keeping the child alive and well, to foster the growth of a child is "to sponsor or nurture [that] child's unfolding, expanding material spirit" (Ruddick 1995, 83). While it would be possible to discuss the application of the goals of preservation and growth to the practice of teaching, I am more interested here in the moral enigma posed by the goal of acceptability. Ruddick states:

> [The mother] must shape natural growth in such a way that her child becomes the sort of adult that she can appreciate and others can accept. Mothers will vary enormously, individually and socially, in the traits and lives they will appreciate in their children. Nevertheless, a mother typically takes as the criterion of her success

---

1 Ruddick construes mothering as work, not as a fixed biological or legal relationship (Ruddick 1995, xi). She is interested in maternal thinking (Ruddick 1995, 31), not just in maternal feelings. A mother's thought is a learned discipline, aimed at a certain conception of achievement, achievement that may not always be realized (Ruddick 1983, 214). Ruddick stresses that her characterization of maternal thought represents an ideal, not necessarily the reality of mothers' actual behaviour (Ruddick 1995, 31).

the production of a young adult acceptable to her group. (Ruddick 1983, 215)

Acceptability, Ruddick tells us, "is defined in terms of the values of the mother's social group—whatever of its values she has internalized as her own plus values of group members whom she feels she must please or is fearful of displeasing" (Ruddick 1983, 220). It is "the primary social groups with which a mother is identified, whether by force, kinship, or choice, [that] demand that she raise her children in a manner acceptable to them" (Ruddick 1995, 17). While a mother often internalizes the values of the social group that determines the acceptability of her offspring, often, too, she may be "ambivalent about her group's values and feel[] alienated or harassed by the group's demands on her and her children" (Ruddick 1995, 21).

Hence, says Ruddick, there is a built-in paradox within maternal thinking:

in response to the demand of acceptability, maternal thinking becomes contradictory—that is, it betrays its own interest in the growth of children.... [M]ost groups and men impose at least some values that are psychologically and physically damaging to children. Yet, to be 'good,' a mother may be expected to endorse these inimical values. (Ruddick 1983, 220, 221)

When social demands for the acceptability of her children conflict with the children's needs for protection and nurturance, the result for the mother is "painful and self-fragmenting conflict" (Ruddick 1995, 22). Ruddick notes that a mother may experience a "fear of the gaze of others" (Ruddick 1995, 112), a fear that results in inauthenticity: "Although they [mothers] teach appropriate behavior, the purposes of that behavior is [*sic*] not theirs to determine" (Ruddick 1995, 112).

Like maternal thinking, pedagogical thinking is, in part, governed not only by the interest of the (intellectual and social) growth of the student, but also by the interest of shaping an acceptable student. The existence of these two interests can generate a paradox, a moral conflict between assisting and denying the student, between advancing the student's development and complicity with academic culture's norms.

As teachers we are subject to the danger Mary McCarthy, in *The Groves of Academe*, refers to as the "insidious egotism of the Potter's Hand, the desire to shape and mold the better-than-common clay and breathe one's own ghostly life into it—the teacher's besetting temptation" (McCarthy 1951, 75). Joyce Garvin confesses, "I suspect that at the soul of our profession lies a wistful but unremitting desire to influence people. (There, I've said it!) It's an urge, not uncommon, to define ourselves by producing a significant impression on others" (Joyce Garvin 1991, 285). In particular, feminist instructors seek to sensitize their students to sexism, misogyny, and masculinism; encourage thoughtful analysis of their sources and meanings; and inspire a determination to resist forms of oppression.

It might seem that academic acceptability is a matter only of conformity to the instructor's own standards and demands. And it is true that just as mothers have real power (Ruddick 1995, 35), power over their children, so also do instructors have real power, power over their students, and we use that power to enforce our norms of acceptability. Nevertheless, within academia there are several other sources of the demand for acceptability.

In addition to the instructor's standards, there are the structures and rules of the university (which has recently been using the term "accountability" to express its demands for acceptability), as well as norms enforced by individuals and institutions external to the university, including alumni/ae, employers and businesses, parents, and politicians. Students themselves can also generate pressures on instructors for certain sorts of acceptability. In lean academic times these pressures are exacerbated by a consumerist mentality on the part of some students who may explicitly demand "what they paid for"—and "what they paid for" may not match the instructor's idea of how the course should be conducted.

These arbiters of acceptability are academic versions of what Ruddick calls Fathers, with a capital "F." Children must submit to and internalize the Law of the Father (Ruddick 1995, 110) as it is enforced by mothers. Similarly, students must submit to and internalize the Law, or Laws, of their department, their faculty, the university administration, the Board of Trustees, and the provincial or state government, as they are enforced by their instructors.

But why should this characteristic of academic life be personally and morally troubling?

My feelings of fraudulence are generated, in part, by an academic system that continues to require behaviours from my students that conflict both with feminist ideals and with what I perceive to be their intellectual, social, and personal growth. Moreover, I am unable to sufficiently change the rules and roles themselves to make the environment more conducive to my students' development. And the university demands my complicity in ensuring the acceptability of students.

Feminist academics have particular reasons to fear the institutional gaze, which not only assesses our behaviour according to standard academic norms, but may even raise silent or not-so-silent questions about our fittingness to be here, about whether we are "real" scholars. Hence we run the risk of being co-opted by our institution; the university itself becomes the audience whose approval determines our speech and our behaviour, and appears to compel us to render our students acceptable in institutional terms.

Every year instructors are required to handle larger and larger classes, mark more and more papers and examinations, serve on more and more committees, and supervise more and more graduate students. The result is that, over-burdened myself, I over-burden my students. I overwork them; make them anxious; and contribute to conditions ripe for cheating, anxiety, and nervous breakdowns. I am part of a system that often manages to take the joy from learning, from reading, from writing and speaking, and turn it into a job, a job that many students are only too happy to dodge in the present or leave behind in the future when they graduate.

For feminists, anti-racists, and other opponents of systemic oppression, the multiple demands of academic acceptability may be irreconcilable with emancipatory moral and political principles. As a result, for the sake of producing acceptable students, and being perceived as acceptable myself, I must struggle to reconcile my feminist principles with my teaching practice. I find myself continuing to inflict examinations, deadlines, and late penalties on my students. I pile work on my students, acting as if my course were the only one they are taking. The course must be rigorous, the reading list formidable. Sometimes I become uncomfortable when students have too-frequent recourse to stories told from their experience, or trade jokes, or fail to engage in a distant abstract theorizing. I cannot send my students, vulnerable and honest, to non-feminist classes where their tendencies to connect theory and practice and to contribute cooperatively to the resolution of problems may render them targets of ridicule. Instead, students must be trained in the rhetorical skills of intellectual attack and self-defence. While we read critiques of the "adversary method" (Moulton 1989) in philosophy, it seems important for them to master it. And just like the critics of feminist philosophy, I find myself asking, is what goes on in my classroom really philosophy?

The situation for the feminist academic is that even as we partly define acceptability in our own feminist terms, we continue, and must continue, to achieve acceptability as defined by the university and its "stakeholders." Just as "Mothers cannot let their children continually get into trouble with people who have the power to hurt them and to withhold what they need" (Ruddick 1995, 114), I cannot let my students get into trouble with academic rules and administrative roles that have the power to hurt their chances and withhold the academic credentials they need.

So the most painful source of my feelings of fraudulence is the institutionally-defined requirement to shape my students toward standards that are not only not of my choosing but, often, are in violation of the feminist principles to which I am morally and politically committed.

Revisioning Fraudulent Feelings

Because the feeling of fraudulence is, in part, generated by the material, intellectual, and political conditions under which we work, there is no easy remedy for it. But there are ways of revisioning fraudulent feelings, ways that may prevent them from undermining our labour as university instructors. Those ways involve seizing the opportunities afforded by the performative nature of our work.

Mary Rose O'Reilly sometimes writes as if the imposter syndrome were a permanent feature of teaching, as if teaching performances are an immutable source of ethical paradox. She says, "If we are being honest and attentive, I think there is always a place of discomfort in our teaching practice, a place of incongruity between our beliefs and our conduct" (O'Reilly 1993, 115).

But she also remarks, "Maybe at certain stages you have to try on a lot of masks until you find one that fits your face, or until you feel comfortable appearing without one (and strong enough to take the consequences)" (O'Reilly 1993, 111). I believe it can be productive to act *as if* you have confidence, *as if* you have authority, *as if* you know what you are doing. Teaching is acting; to be a good teacher is to be a successful actor. "The best we can do is to be conscious about our choices, keep distinguishing in our own minds between the mask and the face: today I will pretend this much, risk this much. Aim to pretend less and less, but don't outrun your strength" (O'Reilly 1993, 111).

Given my concerns about fraudulence, the "as if" approach may seem paradoxical. But it is neither dishonest nor deceptive, for it constitutes my best efforts to represent both what I want to be and what my students want me to be. I need not (and should not) set myself up as infallible or even as an expert. But I can strive to act like what I most long to be: a dedicated scholar-teacher, still eager, still learning, and still committed to my students' growth, despite the institutional obstacles. And eventually my teaching mask can be internalized. The mask actually becomes who I am: I become a teacher with confidence, with authority, even a teacher who knows (a lot of the time, if not always) what she is doing. An actor/teacher is one of my ways of being in the world.

Jane Tompkins says, of academics as former graduate students,

> We became so good at imitating our elders, such expert practitioners at imitating whatever style, stance, or attitude seemed most likely to succeed in the adult world from which we so desperately sought approval that we came to be split into two parts: the real backstage self who didn't know anything and the performing self who got others to believe in its expertise and accomplishments. (Tompkins 1991, 25)

But I think she's overly pessimistic. I doubt that the backstage self is significant. I may (fearfully) believe in it, but only my fearful belief, my guilty sense of fraudulence, keeps it alive. The confident self I present in the classroom is (at least a substantial aspect of) who I am.

And who I am is (a substantial aspect of) what I am teaching. Svinicki says, "The teacher is a model of all that it means to be a scholar. The teacher is also a model of what it means to be a thinking person. We teach not only what we know but *what we are*" (Svinicki 1994, 273, my emphasis).

As an academic I can try to model honesty, thoroughness, commitment to learning, inclusiveness, tolerance, and sensitivity to inequality. I can start to see what I do not so much as acting, as an imposter's performance, but as modelling. This means, in part, grappling authentically and visibly with the existential task of teaching (O'Reilly 1993). I may not succeed in embodying academia's standard for academic competence (and, to the extent that that standard incorporates sexagism, I neither can nor want to embody it). Though I may continue to feel fraudulent, in teaching and modelling a feminist set of values in which I deeply believe, and in encouraging a non-adversarial philosophical method that I know is productive, I am not a fraud.

At the same time, the *feeling* (and it is just a feeling) of being an imposter may help both to keep me honest and to compel the integrity of my performance as instructor. For it is true that what I know is limited; I don't have all the answers, and I can (and must) admit it. Part of my modelling involves sharing my doubts and uncertainties (Collins 1983, 378), acknowledging my weaknesses, admitting my mistakes. This sense of humility can lead to more accurate modelling of what I hope and want my students to be—honest thinkers—and to do—reflect carefully and creatively on the issues, while being cautious about going beyond the evidence they possess.

Yet in extolling academic modelling of a way of being in the classroom, it may seem that I am, in the end, simply endorsing a form of acceptability defined in terms of my own priorities. Can I justify this attempt to shape my students, to make them in some respects like myself?

The answer to this question lies in distinguishing between, on the one hand, the minimal conditions for functioning—mine and my students'—in the classroom, and the more complex cognitive frameworks to which I (perhaps temporarily) adhere. Like Michael Collins, I "have no compunction about indoctrination with respect to such values as honesty and respect for other individuals as human beings. We cannot teach our students well if they plagiarize papers, fake laboratory results, or cheat on examinations. We cannot carry out effective classroom discussions without an atmosphere of respect for others' feelings or a sense of shared humanity" (Collins 1983, 375).[2] What one can do in the classroom is defined by the basic conditions that make teaching and learning possible. Such characteristics as honesty, equity, and respect are part of the *sine qua non* of teaching. I am responsible, with the help of my students, for creating the minimal conditions for participation and communication by all of us. What I can try to model are the minimal conditions for intellectual flourishing of myself and my students; and these conditions legitimately provide the criteria of acceptability for those whom I teach.

As part of the "moral" of Chapter 4, I concluded that the university class is a social organism that grows and develops over time. It's possible, unfortunately, to hinder that growth, but it's also possible to foster it. I want to find means for that personality to develop in a way that promotes mutual respect and learning. Hence it is important for everyone to participate as much as possible.

2   See my discussion in Chapter 4.

From the first day I try to set a precedent of expecting that everyone has a contribution to make and will want and be encouraged to make it.

If to a large extent, as I've also suggested, method is content, that is, part of what is being learned is conveyed by the way it is taught, then the classroom should be a place where difficult issues can be dealt with, intensively, rigorously, but also respectfully. So sexism in the classroom, for example, is entirely out of order, because I can't teach if I'm being undermined as a woman, and I doubt that women students can learn if they are being undermined.[3] (Sexism may undermine the men too, but in a more indirect fashion.)

This emphasis on the minimal conditions for functioning and flourishing in the classroom also offers a way out of, or a way around, the dilemma of audience. The dilemma appeared to give me a choice between honesty about my feminist views, risking audience alienation, and reaching my audience, at the cost of an unacceptable dilution of my real beliefs. But since my role as a feminist instructor allows me to model values of openness, tolerance, and resistance to oppression, and since I am trying to create the minimal conditions for the flourishing of all participants in my classes, then part of my task is to reach my student audience by enabling them to

---

3 Within a sexist environment we cannot have an "open discussion" of the supposed merits and weaknesses of sexist beliefs. For such a discussion would make the competence of women an open question, a subject for debate. But the full, fair, and equal participation of any individual in any debate *presupposes* that individual's competence. For this reason an open discussion, with the participation of women, concerning the putative competence of women, is both conceptually and psychologically impossible; the construction of the issue is incompatible with the women's participation.

engage in their own thinking and reevaluation of belief systems—including mine. Without alienating my student audience, I can show what I genuinely believe about (for example) feminist ethics, by trying to create, in the classroom, the kind of egalitarian, open, and reflective community that exemplifies feminist ideals. To the extent that this is possible, the class, as a functioning intellectual organism, provides ongoing evidence that the feminism about which I teach has real value.

Provided my students contribute to the minimal conditions for our collective flourishing, I need not expect them to agree with all my beliefs. They can grapple with the same issues I have confronted and come to their own judgments; indeed, they can identify new issues that I may not yet have recognized. What I need to communicate is not a set of conclusions, but a set of values and a methodology for generating one's own ideas.

Thus, the performative nature itself of teaching provides a way of revisioning my feelings of fraudulence. The "as if" teaching performance leads to an eventual internalization of the mask I seek to project. Teaching becomes, in large part, the modelling of values that are crucial to the flourishing of all participants in my classroom. And that modelling of values provides a way to subvert at least some of the forces that create feelings of fraudulence.

The humanities classroom is a place where we all—both students and instructor—can learn more about who we are now and who we want to become, both individually and collectively. Through the creation of ideas and theories and the development of respectful academic relationships, we constitute and reconstitute our selves as human beings struggling to understand the meanings of our existence.

And in that endeavour there is nothing fraudulent.

CHAPTER 7

Passing for Normal

For several decades feminists have been emphasizing the ways in which academia can be inhospitable to women. More recently, members of the disability movement have been pointing out that the physical environment of many universities is not adequately adapted to the needs and requirements of disabled persons.

Moreover, the cultural environment in academia can also be unreceptive to disablement. Just as persons from working-class origins are often forced or persuaded to pass as middle class, so also are individuals with disabilities often expected to engage in a form of denial or concealment of their identity.

Background

Disabled feminist Liz Crow states: "the most common cause of impairment[1] amongst women[] is a chronic con-

---

1 "Impairment" is usually defined as damage to bodily organs or structures. "Disability" is usually defined as the absence, loss, disruption, or limitation of capacities considered desirable either by the disabled individual and/or by her culture. Yet there are serious moral and conceptual problems and ambiguities in making the distinction between impairment and disability

dition, arthritis, where the major manifestation of impairment is pain" (Crow 1996, 221). Starting in April 1995, and lasting for over a year, I developed an illness initially diagnosed as rheumatoid arthritis, then re-diagnosed as viral arthritis. As a result of severe pain caused by swelling and inflammation in almost all my joints, I was forced to give up most of my usual activities, including fitness classes, skating, dancing, and even walking. I was weak, anaemic, exhausted, and, even at the height of summer, unable to stay warm. I experienced great pain and difficulty in climbing stairs and opening doors. I could not fasten my own car seat-belt, carry books, open cans and bottles, or lift pots and pans. My life of teaching and research at the university was compromised and curtailed.

I experienced my condition of disablement as being similar to the state of being very old. I do not assume that old people are necessarily disabled. But while I was sick I lived and moved in ways that reminded me of my two grandmothers when they were in their nineties.

Viral arthritis compelled me to engage in what Maria Lugones calls "world-traveling" (Lugones 1989). Lugones introduces the term "world-traveling" to describe her experience of attempting to understand, by identifying with, other women (Lugones 1989, 276), in particular her mother. A world, in Lugones's sense, can be "an actual society given its dominant culture's description and construction of life" (Lugones 1989, 281), or it can be a society or portion of a society given a "nondominant" or "idiosyncratic" construction (Lugones 1989, 282). In other words, a "world" in Lugones's sense is a society or part of

(Bickenbach 1993, 30-47; Wendell 1996, 11-23). I therefore do not make further use of this distinction in this chapter.

a society *as it is interpreted, understood, and lived* by a particular (dominant or non-dominant) group. Lugones recommends world-travelling, in her meaning of the term, as a means of coming to understand what it is to be a person of a different world and "what it is to be ourselves in their eyes" (Lugones 1989, 289). To world-travel, then, is to deliberately immerse and engage oneself in a construction or paradigm of society that is different from one's own, and that is generated by members of a specific social group.

Lugones is interested primarily in race and racism and does not apply her concept of world-travelling to the situation of persons with disabilities. Nonetheless, I find that the concept helps me to understand my experiences with disability. As a person who customarily inhabits the academic world of primarily non-disabled persons, I had almost no comprehension of disablement or of the social climate that helps to create and aggravate the harms associated with disability. I had no recognition of the extent to which the university environment, both physical and social, can be almost uninhabitable for persons with disabilities. But arthritis compelled me to travel to the world of persons with disabilities, and for a time I lived within that world, with all of its socially-constructed limitations and its opportunities for new experiences.[2] Part of what this means, in Lugones's terms, is that I identified with persons with disabilities, and that I was constructed as a person with disabilities.

2 Nancy Mairs writes, "Disability is at once a metaphorical and a material state, evocative of other conditions in time and space—childhood and imprisonment come to mind—yet 'like' nothing but itself" (Mairs 1996, 58).

I am no longer compelled to inhabit the world of persons with disabilities, but I remember the person I was in that world, and I remember some of what I learned while I was there. In this chapter I draw upon part of what I learned. I scrutinize one form of ableist behaviour;[3] namely, the pressure on disabled persons to pass as non-disabled, and the implicit assumptions that underlie and rationalize it. Although this chapter arises out of and is motivated by my experience of temporary disablement, I emphasize that I am adhering to the first of what feminist philosopher Joyce Trebilcot calls her three "methods for using language" (Trebilcot 1994, 43). Her first principle is, "I speak only for myself":

> I speak 'only for myself' not in the sense that only I am my intended audience but, rather, in the sense that I intend my words to express only my own ideas about the world. I expect that some wimmin [*sic*] will find that what I say is more or less true for them too and that some will not. (And that in both groups, some will find my ideas to be useful to them, and others will not.) I want to assume differences and to learn to leave spaces for them. (Trebilcot 1994, 46)

Although I make a number of extrapolations on the basis of my experience of disablement, I do not assume that my experience is necessarily like that of other persons who experience disablement. For, as Nancy Mairs, a disabled

3 Ableism is a complex of beliefs, attitudes, and behaviours reflecting and reinforcing discrimination against and subordination of persons with disabilities. Ableism is founded upon misguided assumptions about the centrality, value, capacities, and normalcy of non-disabled persons.

woman with multiple sclerosis, wisely acknowledges about her own writing, "the range of bodies with disabilities is so exceptionally broad that I could not possibly speak for them all and do not wish to be perceived as trying to do so" (Mairs 1996, 43).

Pressure to Pass

While the disabilities I incurred with viral arthritis were created in part by my unsupportive social and physical environment, much of it located at the university, they were not experientially separable from the pain I suffered. I found that, regardless of the help I received from traditional and alternative therapies, being arthritic was almost continuously unpleasant and uncomfortable. Hence, throughout my illness I wanted to return to a condition of health. There was nothing good about the state I was in (although in retrospect I don't regret that I went through it). For me, then, normalcy came to mean absence of pain, along with the ability to participate in activities—like walking and carrying books—that used to be routine for me.

However, I also experienced, from many people whom I encountered, a strong pressure to *pass* for normal.[4] I define passing as the concealment of a

4   For a discussion of the origins of the concept of normalcy, see Davis 1995, 23-49. Davis says it is "the notion of normalcy that makes the idea of disability (as well as the ideas of race, class, and gender) possible" (Davis 1995, 158). For a discussion of the "disciplines of normality," see Wendell 1996, 87-92.

stigmatized identity,[5] often through the assumption of a counterpart non-stigmatized identity. Despite my disabilities, I was urged to play the role of a non-disabled person. I experienced a pressure not to be ill, not to show weaknesses or to exhibit pain. Some people told me that I was not ill, or that I was getting better, even when I saw no evidence of this, and indeed when my own experience flatly contradicted their assurances. Apparently people find it hard to believe people with disabilities, or to accept that they are trustworthy informants with respect to their own bodily states and conditions. Hence people felt free to disallow my accounts of my own condition.

Even when some colleagues knew about my arthritis they continued to schedule meetings that I was expected to attend in relatively inaccessible locations. Most of all, some faculty and students continued to ask me to do things for them—to join committees, give talks, provide advice, comment on papers and theses, and listen to their troubles—as if I were not ill. This behaviour is a manifestation of the pressure on disabled persons to pass as non-disabled.

Some people used my illness as an opportunity/invitation to present their own experiences of illness and disability or those of a relative. I see this behaviour as a form of pressure on me to pass, because it assumed and required that I was well enough to serve as a counsellor for their distresses about illness. As a variation, people took the opportunity to tell me that, though ill themselves, they were coping much better than I. Unlike me, they did not need to take time off work, or abandon pro-

5 Similarly, some people are also pressured to pass, and may attempt to pass, as white or heterosexual, because being a person of colour and being gay/lesbian/bisexual are stigmatized identities.

fessional commitments, or rest for several hours a day. I interpret these claims as declarations that they were succeeding in passing to a greater degree than I was.

The pressure to pass sometimes manifested itself as a pressure to choose to be well. Some people assumed that I could just heal myself, if only I would try whatever bizarre and esoteric treatment they recommended (cf. Wendell 1996, 97)—which they might never have tried themselves, but had only heard about somewhere. What followed from this belief, of course, was that if I didn't get better it was from failure of effort;[6] hence my pain and ongoing disabilities were my own fault (cf. Morris 1991, 2; Wendell 1996, 27). As Susan Wendell astutely remarks, "When you listen to this culture in a disabled body, you hear how often health and physical vigour are talked about as if they were moral virtues" (Wendell 1989, 113). Moreover, people were only too happy to blame my illness on my way of life. I don't smoke or use illegal drugs, and I drink alcohol only moderately. Hence, many people concluded that my illness was a result of (and perhaps also a punishment for) the intense and incessant labour I have exerted to hold my place in the academic world.[7]

The reason people pass, or attempt to pass, is that there are penalties for possessing or being perceived to possess a stigmatized identity and rewards for success-

6 Partly as a consequence I experienced a fear that I might become permanently disabled if I did not remain at all times positive and optimistic about my chances of recovery.

7 In reality, the necessity for such labour is generated by the sexist belief, still unfortunately prevalent, that women may not be talented enough to hold professional positions in the university; hence, the standards for women's performance often tend to be higher than those for men.

fully presenting oneself as not having it. Barbara Hillyer, a feminist and the mother of a disabled daughter, points out,

> [D]enial of disability is socially sanctioned in that people who valiantly overcome their handicaps are idealized, and the model of good adjustment for everyone in society at large is healthy, physically fit, emotionally well balanced, and mentally alert. (Hillyer 1993, 109)

Thus, passing as non-disabled is, according to Hillyer, the result of "the extreme societal pressure to pass, to act normal, to conform" (Hillyer 1993, 147). A disabled woman remarks,

> The status quo likes us to be seen as 'fighting back', to resent and bewail the fact that we can no longer do things in their way. The more energy and time we spend on over-achieving and compensatory activity that imitates as closely as possible 'normal' standards, the more people are reassured that 'normal' equals right. If we succumb to their temptations they will reward us with their admiration and praise. (Pam Evans, quoted in Morris 1991, 101)

Hillyer suggests that the advantages of passing as non-disabled include not only "survival reasons" but also "political reasons," such as communicating with people who would otherwise reject the message if they knew it came from someone belonging to a "devalued group" (Hillyer 1993, 140). She even suggests that, while the disability movement itself does not advocate passing, it nonetheless indirectly contributes to the pressures and

benefits of passing as non-disabled: "[I]ts stress on pro-
ductivity and even on resisting discrimination may rein-
force individual decisions to pass in order to maintain
employment and to avoid social isolation" (Hillyer 1993,
143).

I see a similarity between the pressure I experienced
to pass as non-disabled and the pressure that Marilyn
Frye says white people exert to insist that light-skinned
people are white:

> The concept of whiteness is not just used, in these cases,
> it is *wielded*. Whites exercise a power of defining who is
> white and who is not, and are jealous of that power....
> [W]hen someone has been clearly and definitely
> decided to be white *by* whites, her claim that she is *not*
> white must be challenged; ... because anyone who is
> even possibly marginal cannot be allowed to draw the
> line. (Frye 1983, 115, her emphasis)

The similarity between this pressure exerted by whites
and the pressure exerted by non-disabled people is that
non-disabled people seek to exercise the power of defining who is disabled and who is not and exert pressure to
pass on persons who might otherwise wish to self-define
as disabled.[8]

Yet passing as non-disabled, like all forms of passing,
exacts a price. Hillyer lists many costs of passing, including
depriving society of knowledge of disablement, "emotive

---

8 I suspect, though this goes beyond my own experience, that non-
disabled persons may sometimes also arrogate to themselves the
right to out those with "hidden" disabilities; that is, to publicly
reveal, against or independently of such persons' will, the
existence in them of disabilities that are ordinarily not readily
perceived.

dissonance" and other harms to the disabled person's psychological and physical health, and complicity in the "oppressive system" that produces the need to pass (Hillyer 1993, 150). Moreover,

> [p]assing—except as a consciously political tactic for carefully limited purposes—is one of the most serious threats to selfhood…. Denial to the outside world and relief at its success … blurs [sic] into denial of self….
> (Cynthia Rich quoted in Morris 1991, 36)

Insofar as I sometimes succumbed to pressure to try to pass as non-disabled, I was colluding with the self-deception of non-disabled others and ultimately contributing to my own self-deception. For, as Baba Copper says, passing "involves lying first to others and ultimately to one's self" (Copper 1988, 18).

Ableism, Ageism, and the Pressure to Pass

There is at least a two-fold connection between ableism and ageism: On the one hand, people who are disabled may be inappropriately treated as if they were either dramatically older or dramatically younger[9] than they actu-

---

9 My uncle, my mother's only brother, has been severely disabled since birth. He cannot speak much, or care for himself. It was only when he was in his sixties and went to live in an institution for disabled adults that my mother realized that Jack had been treated as a little boy all his life. By contrast, the institution's employees recognize him for what he is, a disabled adult, and respect him as such. I conclude that some persons with disabilities are subjected to infantilization. To be infantilized is to be unjustifiably classified as a child and subjected to the political and social treatment thought appropriate to children (Overall 1996).

ally are; on the other hand, people who are ageing are subjected to disablement in a culture that is set up to serve the needs of the young and the non-disabled.

But a further similarity between ableism and ageism is that there are comparable pressures on disabled people and old people to pass. In her book *Over the Hill: Reflections on Ageism Between Women*, Copper challenges the reader: "Women face terrible pressure to hide their disabilities or their age. How do you participate in exerting these pressures?" (Copper 1988, 89). Her suggestion is that both disablement and advancing age are considered to be shameful weaknesses that must be concealed. People of all ages and abilities internalize the negative valuation of age and of disability and, as a result, almost everyone participates in the social conspiracy to pretend that there are no aged or disabled people.

So, just as there is pressure on disabled women to pass as non-disabled, there is also pressure on older women to pass as younger, and they are rewarded if they do. And here we see that sexism interacts both with ageism[10] and ableism. Older women, like disabled women, must attempt to disguise the fact that they have the "wrong" kind of body. "In a society that equates 'vitality' and 'beauty' with physical soundness, a disabled woman must come to terms with serious shortcomings often earlier and even more urgently than others" (Mairs 1996, 128). This phenomenon does not affect only old people. Starting in my teens and lasting until I was about forty, I was consistently rewarded for seeming to be younger than my chronological age. Because sexism interacts with ageism and ableism, the standards for the correct and "desirable"

---

10 Cf. Carpenter's idea of "sexagism," which was discussed in Chapter 6.

form of female body are extremely high, and only the young and non-disabled (and very few of them) have any hope of meeting the requirements.

But the situation is complex. When I was suffering the worst pains and incapacities of my arthritis, I was subjected to punishment for being more disabled than my chronological age would usually predict. To be relatively young (or youngish-looking) and disabled is difficult for others to tolerate. For example, when I attended hydrotherapy at a nearby chronic care hospital I was one of the youngest in the class, but among the most disabled. Yet I consistently experienced resentment, criticism, and impositions from other members of the class. In the women's change room I was expected to be able to stand to dress and undress, and was only grudgingly, if at all, permitted to have a section of the bench on which to sit. I was also regarded as a potential danger to others in the pool: two men made a point of telling me to stay out of their way—even though, unlike some others, I never kicked or walked into another participant.

Therefore, the pressure on me to pass as non-disabled seemed to be exacerbated by a form of ageism. Even persons who are disabled themselves are susceptible to ageism in their reactions to others with disabilities. From the point of view of both disabled and non-disabled persons, disability may be easier to recognize and tolerate (when it is recognized and tolerated at all) in older people than in younger ones.

Underlying Assumptions

Why did many people pressure me to pass as non-disabled? I can only speculate about the causes. Perhaps my illness brought out people's fears. "Other people's pain is always frightening, primarily because people want to deny that it could happen to them," says Jenny Morris (Morris 1991, 101). Disabilities bring intimations of mortality. The shameful status of being old, weak, or ill, and the intimate tie between ableism and ageism, ensure that many people cannot tolerate being near those who are old or sick.

I suggest that two metaphysical assumptions—that is, two implicit and non-empirical presuppositions about the fundamental nature of reality—underlie this culture's insistence that disabled people pass, and serve as a justificatory prop for practices that pressure people to deny that they are ill or disabled.

The first metaphysical assumption is that identities—particularly subordinated and disadvantaged identities—are totalizing; that is, they are assumed to define or constitute the totality of what one is. Lennard J. Davis points out, "Disabled people are thought of primarily in terms of their disability, just as sexual preference, gender, or ethnicity becomes the defining factor in perceiving another person" (Davis 1995, 10). Thus, a gay man is defined by his sexuality, a woman by her gender, a person of colour by his or her race, and a disabled person by disability. Definition by one such characteristic is assumed to exclude the possibility of others. For example, as Shelley Tremain observes, disabled persons are assumed to be asexual; hence people cannot conceive of the existence of disabled dykes (Tremain 1996, 15).[11] If one is disabled, then that is all one is, but to be well is not considered to be a specific identity and hence is not totalizing; it is a blank page on which a large variety of characteristics can be inscribed.

People therefore pressured me to pass because in their view, if I failed to be non-disabled, then disabled is all I would be. My attempts to present myself as disabled and also to have other identities—writer, philosophy instructor, and so on—were sometimes met with disbelief and rejection. I was not permitted to have it both ways. As Wendell remarks, "most non-disabled people cannot wrap their minds around the possibility that someone can be disabled or ill and also work productively, have intimate relationships, or be happy" (Wendell 1996, 4). Because disability is taken to be all-encompassing, it is believed to allow no room for any other identity.

> The term 'disability,' as it is commonly and professionally used, is an absolute category without a level or threshold. One is either disabled or not. One cannot be a little disabled any more than one can be a little pregnant. (Davis 1995, 1)

---

11 Mairs writes:

> Most people ... deal with the discomfort and even distaste that a misshapen body arouses by dissociating that body from sexuality in reverie and practice. 'They' can't possibly do it, the thinking goes; therefore, 'they' mustn't even want it; and that is *that* (Mairs 1996, 51, her emphasis).

One possible explanation for this phenomenon is connected to ageism: "In this culture people with disabilities are expected to be perpetual children which means that sexual expression would not be appropriate and may be considered perverted" (Pat Danielson, quoted in Mairs 1996, 140).

On the basis of this metaphysical assumption, if disabled was not everything that I was, then I could not be (truly) disabled.

I believe that to combat this metaphysical assumption, disabled persons face a struggle comparable to that faced by feminists with respect to the concept of woman. On the one hand, feminists insist that to *be* a woman *matters*—politically, epistemically, socially, and ethically. Being gendered female in this culture affects virtually every aspect of one's life, and it provides the pretext for stereotyping and injustice by other people. On the other hand, feminists insist that to be considered as *only* a woman, or to assume that that is all a woman is, that she can be understood entirely by virtue of her womanhood, is a metaphysical error. That is, it is a mistake about the nature or reality of women: the mistake of taking female-ness to constitute the entirety of each woman's identity. Being a woman is not so all-consuming that it precludes similarities with those who are not women; women and men are as much alike as they are different.

Similarly, as a temporarily disabled person I wanted to insist that disablement matters—politically, epistemically, socially, and ethically. To be disabled in this culture affects virtually every aspect of one's life, and it provides the pretext for stereotyping and injustice by other people. On the other hand, to be considered *only* a person with disabilities, or to assume that that is all I was, that I could be understood entirely by virtue of my disabilities, was a metaphysical error. Disablement does not constitute the totality of the disabled person's identity. And being disabled is not so all-consuming that it precludes similarities with those who are not disabled; disabled people are as much like non-disabled people as they are different from them (Mairs 1996, 11).

The second metaphysical assumption is that all disabled persons inevitably make demands upon those who are non-disabled, and that disabled persons are not capable of helping others and will renege on their (ascribed) obligations.

This assumption stems from an egoist reference: people pressured me to pass because otherwise my disablement seemed to make some demand on them. They didn't always know what it was, but they usually weren't willing to meet it. Thus Mairs says that she feels "constrained to be a 'good cripple,' cheerful and patient, so that whoever might roll along in my wake someday will find the way eased ..." (Mairs 1990, 73). "[I]n order to earn a shot at social intercourse with 'normals,'" a disabled person "must never publicly lament her state, must preferably never even mention it" (Mairs 1996, 7). Lois Keith points out that disabled people, especially disabled women, are expected to be cheerful and uncomplaining:

> Like many women, Michele [a disabled woman] felt that with her bright smile and sparkling eyes, it was her responsibility to make everything alright [*sic*]. But our desire to make everything easier for ourselves by always being bright and pleasant in our dealings with the world and our need to have everyone think well of us, can be destructive. (Keith 1996, 85)

This pressure, originating both externally and internally, to be "bright and pleasant" is harmful to the moral integrity, psychological harmony, and epistemological clarity of persons with disabilities. I suggest that what lies behind the insistence on cheerfulness is the fear that disabled people are needy and demanding; being "bright and pleasant" helps to reassure non-disabled people that disabled persons won't make heavy demands on them—or that if we do, we'll be bright-eyed and appreciative about any response we get. So ironically, far from making demands on people, disabled women often end up being, and having to be, concerned about others' feelings, trying to reduce the threat we apparently constitute to the non-disabled.[12] Care for others' feelings is a typical component of "women's work," and the social need for it is as intense, if not more so, when the woman is disabled.

Just as important, people feared that I wouldn't do for them what they wanted, or take care of them in ways they usually expected. Non-productivity, even outright uselessness, is automatically coupled both with disability and with ageing. As Copper says, "no matter what old women do or don't do, they are seen as non-productive"

---

12 I am reminded of a comment by a black graduate student, David Sealey, who said he felt he had to "take care of" white people who feel threatened by his skin colour; in particular, to be sensitive and careful about whites' feelings.

It might be argued that white people and non-disabled people may have comparable experiences, feeling that they may be or be perceived as a threat to people of colour and to disabled people, and hence feeling obliged to treat these "others" with extra sensitivity. There is, however, an important difference between the significance of these feelings as they are experienced by members of marginalized groups, and their significance as they are experienced by members of dominant groups, for people in marginalized groups are already dealing with serious disadvantages. To add the requirement of sensitivity to and care for the feelings of people in the dominant groups simply exacerbates their burdens—and, arguably, reinforces their oppression.

(Copper 1988, 79). There is a similar perception of people with disabilities (Mairs 1996, 62). In my own case, I suspect this reaction was especially acute for two reasons: first, caring for others is an ongoing expectation made of women,[13] even (or especially) academic women. We are required to function as professional "mothers" within the institution, and mothers are expected to be entirely oriented to the needs and desires of others. Second, as one of the few full professors (and even fewer female full professors) at my academic institution, I am perceived as being particularly powerful. Neediness and vulnerability are not recognized in people who are thought to wield institutional power. The threat posed by my arthritis of a potential failure to exert my power was therefore especially frustrating to other people. The pressure on me to pass as non-disabled was, in part, people's way of trying to ensure that I would continue to assist them in the ways they expected.

To combat this second metaphysical assumption, that all disabled persons inevitably make demands on the non-disabled, and that the disabled are incapable of adhering to their moral obligations, disabled persons face a tough challenge. We must simultaneously strive to ensure that our legitimate needs are met; to reject the demand that we necessarily be cheerful and grateful; and, especially in the case of women, not to be coerced by others' distress if we fail to serve their wants.

---

13 My experience is like that of Wendell, who says, "the subculture of feminists of my generation is one of self-sacrifice. Good feminists, like good women everywhere, are supposed to give 'til it hurts ..." (Wendell 1996, 4). This expectation contributes to the feminist "role muddles" I discussed in Chapter 2.

While in many cases we can continue to function as contributing members of our institutions and cultures (and that fact must be recognized), we also have to ensure that the changing needs and requirements created by our disablement are not overlooked, denied, or rejected. To individuals who are not disabled, this complex of demands may seem paradoxical. For we are asking non-disabled persons both to accept that, because of disablement, we may not be able to continue with our ordinary tasks and duties, and also to acknowledge that because each of us is more than her disability, we should not be assumed to be totally incapacitated. In other words, disabled people need to find a way to encourage non-disabled persons to recognize that persons with disabilities are not uni-dimensional. Just like non-disabled persons, disabled people possess a full range of characteristics and capacities. To be disabled is not to be consumed by disability.

Final Comments

In this chapter I have described the pressure on disabled persons to pass as non-disabled, indicated some of its connections with ageist and sexist pressures to pass as young and conventionally attractive, and presented what I take to be the assumptions that rationalize the pressure to pass as non-disabled. For disabled persons, as for anyone with a stigmatized identity (such as people of colour, lesbians, gays, and bisexuals, and old people), to choose not to pass requires confidence, energy, and courage.

In writing this discussion I was surprised to discover, by contrast to my feelings in assessing the problems of sexism, how little optimism I could summon about the dismantling of ableism. Unlike my approach in earlier chapters, here I am not able to provide neat solutions or clear revisionings for these problems of prejudice. Perhaps it is because the experience of disability is so recent, and contrasts so powerfully with my life, before and since, of non-disability.

While no longer disabled, I remain determined to hang on to the insights that disability afforded me. No longer do I take good health, abundant energy, and easy mobility for granted; I appreciate and feel grateful for them all. I possess vivid memories of the forbidding and obstructive nature of the physical environment—steps to climb, door knobs to twist, heavy doors to push or pull open, slippery sidewalks to negotiate in winter—and I now recognize how inaccessible are our human and natural surroundings. Because of these memories, I hope that my former ignorance about the situation of persons with disabilities has been permanently compromised.

In reflecting about my experiences I was also surprised to uncover the anger I felt in response to the pressure to pass as non-disabled. I remain outraged that people could not just let me be, to heal in my own time. I am angry that they tried to remake me into their image of who I most usefully could be for them. The pressure to pass for normal, to play the role of non-disabled academic, was never a helpful component of my recovery from viral arthritis. As Mairs points out, it is

> the normally unconscious attitudes that chill the social climate for people marked out by disability. Although these do not threaten bodily harm, they deplete and shrivel the spirit, leaving people whose resources may

already be scanty enough hollowed out and sad. (Mairs
1996, 99)

I conclude that while people with disabilities are expected to meet high moral standards, a major moral defect—
the inability to accept and support persons with disabilities—continues to pass for normal among many people
who are non-disabled.

CHAPTER 8

Personal Histories, Social Identities, and Feminist Philosophical Inquiry

The Case for Using Personal Histories and Social Identities

Where does philosophy come from?

The work of individual philosophers is not just the product of an impersonal quest, responding to the objective demands of truth or the inherent interest of certain issues. Out of an indefinitely large set of philosophical concepts, claims, theories, and problems a philosopher must select. Philosophical labour arises in part from individual assessments of what is important, what is controversial, and what is worth investigating, all of which derive from who we are, what we assume, and what we value. That is, philosophical inquiry is in part an expression of one's personal history.

But feminist philosophers have also argued[1] that philosophy is an expression not just of individual history, but of the social identity of the philosopher—that is, his or her cultural embodiment as a member of a gender class, a race, and a socio-economic class. As Susan Bordo puts

---

[1] The arguments have been made in various forms by Clark and Lange (1979), Ruth (1981), Harding and Hintikka (1983), Lloyd (1984), and Le Doeuff (1990), among others.

it, since the advent of the feminist critique, philosophical ideas can "no longer claim to descend from the heavens of pure rationality or to reflect the inevitable and progressive logic of intellectual or scientific discovery," but must be recognized instead as "the products of historically situated individuals with very particular class, race, and gender interests" (Bordo 1990, 137). Hence, philosophical concepts, claims, theories, and problems are generated not just by unique and detached personal assessments made by independent philosophers, but also by the social conventions, experiences, priorities, and demographic characteristics of cohorts of philosophers who influence and are influenced by each other.

Non-feminist philosophers have often made liberal use of their own personal experiences (Isaacs-Doyle 1998, 3). For example, that redoubtable contributor to the philosophical canon, René Descartes, treats his experiences of sitting by the fire in his dressing gown, experiencing doubt, as the origin of his meditations on the possibility of knowledge (Descartes [1642] 1985, 18). But feminist philosophy makes explicit the personal nature of much philosophizing, by reminding us that it comes from real people, who use their experiences—their histories and identities—to create philosophy, regardless of whether they are conscious of, or acknowledge, its sources and its limitations.

What conditions permit some philosophers to ignore or deny the personal, experientially-based nature of their philosophy? If almost everyone in an area of human endeavour is the same or similar with respect to such key social identities as gender, race, or class status,[2] then the

---

2 Or age, health status or disability, or sexual orientation.

significance of those features becomes difficult or impossible to recognize. If one is the norm, one can take oneself for granted, and one is taken for granted by others. When maleness, whiteness, and material privilege are normal, as they have been, until very recently, virtually everywhere in academia, then they appear uninteresting, unworthy of comment, and even imperceptible.

But for members of minority groups, among whom I include women in academia, it is much harder, often even impossible, to ignore who one is. Describing the early history of feminist women in academia, Bordo states, "[T]o be a feminist academic was to be constantly aware of one's Otherness; one could not forget that one was a woman even if one tried. The feminist imagination was fueled [*sic*] precisely by what it was never allowed to forget" (Bordo 1990, 148).

I believe this condition still prevails today. We minority group members are seen as bodies, as deviant bodies with specific identities,[3] and we are present in the university classroom, lecture hall, or library as bodies with identities, whether we like it or not. For the minority group member, "[t]he insistence of the personal preexists the decision to engage in the practice of self-inclusion, the politics of the personal. Indeed, the minority teacher

---

3   bell hooks is especially clear about this:

> [A]s a black woman, I have always been acutely aware of the presence of my body in those settings that, in fact, invite us to invest so deeply in a mind/body split so that, in a sense, you're almost always at odds with the existing structure, whether you are a black woman student or professor. But if you want to remain, you've got, in a sense, to remember yourself—because to remember yourself is to see yourself always as a body in a system that has not become accustomed to your presence or to your physicality (hooks 1994, 135).

is already known *in personal terms* ..." (Karamcheti 1995, 138, her emphasis). In other words, the identification of the minority group individual as a particular kind of body (rather than generally, as a person or as mind) precedes and inevitably influences any attempt she may make to participate in the activities and institutions of the dominant culture. Because we are seen as exemplars of our gender, our class, our sexuality, and/or our race, we (must) become aware both of our personal histories and of our social identities:

> Until the advent of feminist philosophy, modern philosophers had rarely considered what effect their gender—and many other aspects of their embodiment —had on their philosophizing.... It was at first startling and then empowering to learn that, whatever our philosophical credentials, we [female philosophers] were seen or thought of as experiencing the world first and foremost as *women*, while males, especially male philosophers, were seen or thought of as experiencing the world as subjects, knowers, doers, or agents. (McAlister and Waugh 1997, viii)

If I am not the norm, I have at least two choices. I can attempt to minimize my differences and make myself, as far as possible, like the norm, hoping that I will be accepted as just one mind labouring among other minds.[4] Or, I can accept or at least recognize my differences, in

---

4 As Michele Le Doeuff remarks, "Often we feel we are in the opposite position to that of Scheherazade: she had to keep telling fascinating tales to prevent herself from being murdered by her mad husband, while we are 'annihilated' as women when we manage to make people listen to us" (Le Doeuff 1990, 159).

body, background, and/or culture—differences that others are unlikely to let me forget—and investigate their meaning and the ways in which such differences may be either liabilities or benefits.

To do philosophy as a woman or as a member of some other minority group does not result in a unitary or predictable philosophical method or content. But it does mean, at a minimum, that one is more likely to use personal history and social identity both as inspiration for philosophical ideas and as a heuristic for the generation of philosophical method. The material base for this likelihood lies in the social conditions that make it difficult for minority group members to ignore who they are, that draw attention to an alleged discrepancy between academic role on the one hand and political and/or cultural identity on the other.

For some philosophers, then, the explicit philosophical use of personal history and social identity is rendered plausible, if not inevitable, by one's peculiar situation as a minority among philosophers. Minority status often results in a kind of self-consciousness—not through any inherent wisdom or epistemic insight of the minority group person, but because a deviant social status tends to create self-consciousness.[5] Marilyn Frye astutely observes,

> One of the privileges of being normal and ordinary is a certain unconsciousness. When one is that which is

---

5 This idea is closely connected to feminist standpoint epistemology, the theory that marginalized social positions offer the possibility of a better and more complete understanding of social reality than that which is afforded by positioning among those who are socially dominant. See, for example, Hartsock 1983; Harding 1986, 1990, and 1993; Bar On 1993; Longino 1993; and Collins 1996.

taken as the norm in one's social environment, one does not have to think about it... If one is the norm, one does not have to know what one is. If one is marginal, one does not have the privilege of not noticing what one is.

This absence of privilege is a presence of knowledge. As such, it can be a great resource, given only that the marginal person does not scorn the knowledge and lust for inclusion in the mainstream, for the unconsciousness of normalcy. (Frye 1983, 147)

This feminist recognition of the relationships between philosophy and the persons who philosophize constitutes a *prima facie* case for the explicit invocation of personal history and social identity within philosophical inquiry, especially feminist philosophical inquiry. In practical terms, it mandates the explicit and aware use of personal experiences within the classroom and within scholarly writing—the employment of stories that begin, "I feel," "I remember," "I perceive," "I value," "I need," and even "I am."

Moreover, feminists have historically relied upon an appeal to personal experiences such as these, both in theory and in practice. Many believe that the invocation of experience, at least as a heuristic, is necessary to feminist research and learning.[6] As a feminist philosopher I am committed to the basic feminist idea, "The personal is political," and to its corollary, that the personal can be both educational and of scholarly significance, a resource for generating and applying concepts, evaluating view-

---

6 One interesting example is Sue Middleton's *Educating Feminists: Life Histories and Pedagogy* (1993).

points (Sherwin 1988), and pointing to political change. As Linda Alcoff remarks, "the category 'woman' needs to be theorized through an exploration of the experience of subjectivity" (Alcoff 1988, 421). Our social identities are "taken (and defined) as a political point of departure, as a motivation for action, and as a delineation of [our] politics" (Alcoff 1988, 431-432).

The feminist case for appealing to personal histories and social identities within teaching and research therefore appears straightforward. As Jane Tompkins puts it, describing her own academic goals: "I wanted to change the way it was legitimate to behave inside academic institutions…. I wanted never to lose sight of the fleshly, desiring selves who were engaged in discussing hegemony or ideology or whatever it happened to be…" (Tompkins 1991, 27). Starting from our own experiences, inside and outside the classroom, seems both more honest and more authentic. It appears to offer a way to avoid the alienation that traditional pedagogy and scholarship sometimes produce, and it promises to obviate the bifurcation of theory and "real life" so often attributed to ivory tower academics.

The appeal to personal history and social identity, especially in the lecture hall and the classroom, is also a way of dispersing power and refraining from the promulgation of Truth with a capital T. It rejects what Tompkins (1991) calls the "performance model" of teaching,[7] and situates education within the students, at least partially deposing the instructor from her professorial throne. It is part of what bell hooks calls "teaching to

---

7 See Chapter 6 for a discussion of teaching as performance and the performance model of teaching.

transgress," that is, education that enables students (and instructors) to reevaluate and reject social norms that reproduce inequality:

> If we want individuals of either gender to understand the ways in which they can be empowered by feminist thinking and politics in everyday life, we have to be willing to overcome a certain protectionism around private experience, to be willing to share concretely what we do and how we do it. What are our habits of being, and what is the impact of feminist thinking on behaviour?... Sharing the personal is also about sharing power. (hooks with McKinnon 1996, 823)

hooks recognizes that the instructor's use of personal experience, her own and that of her students, has the potential for making the classroom more democratic, by breaking down the mystique that makes the instructor seem less fallible than those whom she teaches.

Finally, in light of both theoretical and practical illustrations of the moral and epistemic errors that may arise from speaking for others, or attempting to justify generalizations about groups of women, let alone about women as a whole, personal experience would seem to be one's only true resource, all that one can legitimately speak of—especially if one is a privileged, middle-class white woman. Both charges of essentialism (Alcoff 1988, Martin 1994), and gender scepticism (Bordo 1988, 1990)—that is, doubts about the possibility of using gender as an analytical category—make it seem as if it is seldom safe or even possible to generalize.[8] In Ardis's terms, it appears I must therefore resort to "a discourse that evokes the historical and material conditions of its own production" (Ardis 1992, 174). That is, I must use a language that renders explicit the context and history in and from which it was produced.

Moral, Political, and Epistemological Problems of Appealing to Personal Histories and Social Identities

But despite this *prima facie* and perhaps naive case for using personal history and social identity, these appeals to experience are fraught with problems in the academic setting.[9] They generate epistemological, moral, and political questions for the classroom and for scholarship. The general epistemological question concerns what degree, if any, of legitimate authority is to be granted to individual personal experience. The general ethical and political questions concern the moral justification and political effectiveness, for liberationist goals, of the use of

---

8 Bordo says,

> If generalization is only permitted in the *absence* of multiple
> inflections or interpretive possibilities, then cultural general-
> izations of *any* sort—about race, about class, about historical
> eras—are ruled out. What remains is a universe composed
> entirely of counterexamples, in which the way men and
> women see the world is purely as *particular* individuals, shaped
> by the unique configurations that form that particularity
> (Bordo 1990, 151, her emphasis; cf. Bordo 1988, 629).

9 For a real-life case study in these problems see Shalit 1998.

experience, personal history, and identity within feminist philosophical teaching and writing.[10]

The specific problems arising from using personal experience include the obvious: the dangers of self-indulgence, narcissism, voyeurism (Bernstein 1992, 137), and the violation of privacy—my own and others'; the fear of self-revelation;[11] and even the possibility of boredom.[12]

But the problems also include more insidious dangers. First, what I call "therapism": using the revelation of personal history as a pseudo-therapy in the classroom and in writing. Some academics, with Foucauldian antecedents, have worried that the recounting of experiences, presented as a form of "confession," is punitive of students (cited in hooks 1994, 21). Students may be or feel compelled both to expose what they do not wish to expose, and to shape their own narratives toward the instructor's uses.

Second, there is the possibility that personal experience is not a heuristic but becomes a substitute both for

10 Diana Fuss expresses well part of the dilemma posed by using personal experiences within the classroom:

Personal consciousness, individual oppressions, lived experience—in short, identity politics—operate in the classroom both to authorize and to de-authorize speech (Fuss 1989, 113). How are we to negotiate the gap between the conservative fiction of experience as the ground of all truth-knowledge and the immense power of this fiction to enable and encourage student participation? (Fuss 1989, 118).

11 Jane Tompkins remarks, "I think people are scared to talk about themselves, that they haven't got the guts to do it" (Tompkins 1989, 123).

12 As Ann Ardis admits, "I cannot assume that my autobiographical remarks will be of interest to readers, let alone that they will be considered a theoretical intervention" (Ardis 1992, 173).

philosophical theory[13] and for feminist political action. The appeal to personal history and social identity can be conservative, conventional (Bernstein 1992, 121),[14] apolitical (hooks 1988, 105-111), or de-politicizing (Fuss 1989, 101, 114-117). As Elisabeth Young-Bruehl insists, "[I]dentity is not insight. And autobiography that ends where it began, that defensively or offensively armors an identity rather than journeys in search of one, is simply a weapon, not an education" (Young-Bruehl 1991, 17). In some cases, it has been argued, to invoke the experiences of women, especially marginalized women, is to succumb to co-optation by mainstream culture and academia. It is "to cooperate with our own commodification, to buy from and sell back to the dominant culture its constitution of our always already essentialized identity" (duCille 1994, 606), by trading in the public portrayal of women, and particularly minority women (black, lesbian, disabled, etc.), as a consumable product.

And whose experience gets used? In the classroom, if the instructor's personal history is used, there is a danger that education can turn into a cult of personality or a celebration of the instructor's own habits and predilections

---

13 Susan Wendell wisely expresses the dangers to philosophical theory as follows:

> Philosophy about human beings and human lives always carries the danger of overgeneralizing. Refusing to generalize avoids that danger only at the cost of limiting one's thoughts to meditation on an individual, usually oneself (Wendell 1996, 6).

The question is whether it is possible to philosophize in a way that avoids both dangers.

14 As Susan David Bernstein aptly puts it, the confessional mode can become "a matter of style, a renovation rather than a reformation" (Bernstein 1992, 131).

(cf. Talbot 1994). There is no doubt that the personal experience of even the most versatile and imaginative instructor is a finite resource. Despite the fact that, in Ardis's words, "students often want to position a teacher as a native informant because that's the easiest way for them to account for a teacher's authority *vis à vis* her subject matter" (Ardis 1992, 168),[15] one cannot and should not construct courses, even feminist courses, out of one's own life, because, among other reasons, they would fall into what Jane Roland Martin calls the trap of false generalization.[16] Paradoxically, then, while the turn to personal histories is in part caused and motivated by a determination to avoid inappropriate generalizations that ignore the implications of social identities, personal experience itself is liable to be used in the same way; that is, as a source of unjustified universalizations.

If the aim is to encourage the presentation of students' experiences, there are problems of ownership and appropriation. While it may be legitimate for me to take

---

15 Ironically, the validation of the use of experience in the classroom, with its almost inevitable evocation of identity categories, can also generate problems with respect to one's credibility as a teacher in those cases where the teacher attempts, in Katherine Mayberry's felicitous phrase, to "teach what she is not" (Mayberry 1996), that is, to teach about aspects of women's lives—sexual orientations, races, classes, and so on—that she has not personally experienced.

16 Martin writes:

[I]n the early phase of the late twentieth-century women's movement it was the discovery that the experience of others was so like one's own that was at once comforting, illuminating, and energizing. Sadly, it has turned out that this presumed discovery was a mere invention. Not only were we generalizing from too homogeneous a sample, we also were assuming that those who are alike in some respects are alike in all (Martin 1994, 646).

risks with using my own autobiography, I am not entitled to pre-empt others', or to require that students make use of their experiences when they do not wish to do so. Moreover, the autobiographical turn may be safely available only to the secure and self-confident few. The appeal to the personal in the classroom and in scholarship can result in the privileging of some forms of experience—the instructor's, the scholar's (especially, perhaps, the tenured scholar's [Bernstein 1992, 126]), that of certain dominant groups (Fuss 1989, 68), or even that of certain minority groups (Fuss 1989, 116). Reliance upon the authority of experience can exert a normative effect upon students and upon the dynamism of the classroom, undermining non-experiential arguments, and casting doubt upon those who would call into question the conclusions that experience is used to demonstrate.

Another problem is that within some academic contexts, a lone member of a minority group may be made to become the "native informant" (hooks 1994, 43) for an entire identity group. Whether or not the minority group member seeks it, approves it, or even recognizes it, she is made to stand in as knowledge source and authority for the conditions, beliefs, values, and culture of the group to which she putatively belongs. The creation of such a "native informant" has, once again, the consequence of premature and inappropriate universalization, for while it is epistemically impossible for one person to speak on behalf of an entire group, her statements and accounts of experience may be taken by the class to be, and may even be endorsed by her as being, representative of all those with the same social identity. Moreover, the role of "native informant" puts the minority group member in an untenable position as model representative and exemplar rather than as an individual.

On the other hand, appealing to, and privileging, personal histories of certain kinds may also lead to the sort of "chilly climate" in feminist teaching that Martin identifies in feminist research (Martin 1994): it runs the risk of precluding genuinely valuable generalizations and all uses of general concepts. The retreat to the singular—for example, in a panicked response to pressure by minority group feminists not to talk about white, heterosexual, middle-class women as if they stood for all women—means that the dangers of over-generalization are replaced by the dangers of failing to notice tendencies, patterns, and commonalities (cf. Bordo 1990).

The use of personal history and social identity may also incur personal costs. In some academic contexts, the deployment of personal experience in the classroom may compromise the instructor's reputation or security. As hooks wryly remarks, "One of the ways you can be written off quickly as a professor by colleagues who are suspicious of progressive pedagogy is to allow your students, or yourself, to talk about experience" (hooks 1994, 148). It may also affect students' own academic future. Some argue that the psychological costs for some students of probing their own experiences may be too high (Shalit 1998). My worry is that academic practices of discussion, disclosure, and engagement that students learn in my classroom, practices that they seem to enjoy and value, may nonetheless compromise their ability to function within more conventional classrooms that are suspicious of the role of personal experience.[17]

---

17 As I pointed out in Chapter 6, these worries can contribute to the feeling of fraudulence.

Some academics are also sceptical about the use of personal history and social identity within scholarly research. As Tompkins puts it,

> The problem is that you can't talk about your private life in the course of doing your professional work. You have to pretend that epistemology, or whatever you're writing about, has nothing to do with your life, that it's more exalted, more important, because it (supposedly) *transcends* the merely personal. (Tompkins 1989, 122, her emphasis)[18]

This is a convention that even feminists confront and by which we can be circumscribed and disciplined.[19] Susan David Bernstein suggests that confessional writing is, for some academics, "a source of embarrassment that provokes the gendered charge of emotionalism and anti-intellectualism threatening to reverse recent strides of feminists from the confessional venues of kitchen table-talk and diary entries" (Bernstein 1992, 123). Here's an example of this reaction from my own academic life: a

---

18 Cf. Patricia Williams:

> The other thing contained in assumption of neutral, impersonal writing styles is the lack of risk.... [T]he personal is not the same as 'private': the personal is often merely the highly particular. I think the personal has fallen into disrepute as sloppy because we have lost the courage and the vocabulary to describe it in the face of the enormous social pressure to 'keep it to ourselves.'... (Williams 1991, 93)

19 As I have found to my chagrin, using one's personal life in one's work can give others opportunities for misinterpretation. After I wrote and published an earlier version of Chapter 5, about my experiences as an academic from a working-class background (Overall 1995), I learned that it inspired a rumour that I do not like middle-class students—a claim that is not true and that I have never made.

paper of mine (eventually accepted for publication) was described by one referee as being fatally weakened by my use of "self-centered and arrogant counter examples." These counter examples were simply drawn from my own experience.[20] (It seems ironic that criticisms of my use of personal experience are sometimes themselves intensely personal and, indeed, *ad feminam* in nature.)

Moreover, the appeal to primarily autobiographical accounts can be misleading, if they are taken to represent the essence of what certain people or groups are like. There are two dangers: autobiography appears to posit as essential what is really historical, and it may promote defences of the history rather than an understanding and analysis of it (Edward Said, in Fuss 1989, 115). Within the context of an uncritical deployment of experience, a justifiably outdated foundationalism rears its head, this time with personal experience appearing as an epistemological "trump card" that terminates philosophical argument (Lauritzen 1997, 96). While the appeal to first-person experience appears to endow the "I" with privileged access to its own meanings (Bernstein 1992, 121, 127), the early naive feminist celebration of personal experience for its own sake and in its own terms has, rightly, given way

20 My experientially-based publications have sometimes evoked the claim that what I am doing is not philosophy at all, an effective exclusionary charge and one to which I am only too vulnerable (cf. Sherwin 1988). What could be worse than to fail to produce work that qualifies for the safe bounds of one's own discipline? Another form of dismissal that my experientially-based work has received is that it is popularized, that is, directed to and received by a general, non-philosophical audience. Some scholars apparently believe that to do publicly accessible philosophical work is necessarily to compromise one's academic integrity, by producing work that is sub-standard and/or not "real" scholarship.

to a rueful understanding that experience itself is mediated by human symbol-making and is partly an ideological product generated by prevailing concepts and values (Fuss 1989, 25; Bernstein 1992, 122). No experience or set of experiences provides incontestable or indubitable access to reality, patriarchal or otherwise, and no experience or set of experiences implies or compels any one definitive interpretation or evaluation. As Paul Lauritzen expresses it,

> there is a danger in appealing to experience that experience gets naturalized in a way that precludes examining how experience is produced.... [R]elying on experience creates a tendency to accept a self-authenticating subjectivity, which does not adequately acknowledge the fact that, far from explaining or justifying particular moral [and other] claims, 'experience' may be the reality in need of explanation. (Lauritzen 1997, 94)

Solutions/Resolutions

In the course of grappling with the moral, political, and epistemological problems raised by the use of experiences in feminist teaching and research, I believed and hoped that a neat solution or a set of neat solutions would reveal itself. For, as I demonstrate throughout this book, I make liberal use of experience, my own and others', in my teaching and research; I wanted to be able to justify, in *post hoc* fashion, what I already do. hooks expresses well the delicate path I wanted to tread:

I am troubled by the term 'authority of experience', acutely aware of the way it is used to silence and exclude. Yet I want to have a phrase that affirms the specialness of those ways of knowing rooted in experience. I know that experience can be a way to know and can inform how we know what we know. Though opposed to any essentialist practice that constructs identity in a monolithic, exclusionary way, I do not want to relinquish the power of experience as a standpoint on which to base analysis or formulate theory. (hooks 1994, 90)

As I wrote this book the problems for feminist philosophical inquiry of appealing to personal history and social identity seemed to multiply. Yet I continued to believe, on the basis of my own pedagogical and scholarly practices and observation, that using experiences within philosophical teaching and writing is justified.

In her gentle yet challenging book, *The Peaceable Classroom*, Mary Rose O'Reilly responds to the criticism that experiential learning could turn her English class into "some kind of therapy session":

'Some kind of therapy session': now why do we use that phrase in a pejorative sense—as though we do not need all the help we can get?... I would like to meet the concern about turning the classroom into 'some kind of therapy group' ... by observing that good teaching *is*, in the classical sense, therapy: good teaching involves reweaving the spirit. (Bad teaching, by contrast, is soul murder.) (O'Reilly 1993, 46-47, her emphasis)

So why do I continue to deploy personal history and social identity in teaching and research? I propose a sort of pragmatic/activist response. I use it because, as I have tried to show throughout *A Feminist I*, it works. Because it moves people, fosters connections, and develops philosophical understanding and imagination. Because some of the most powerful, enlightening, and *whole*some feminist philosophy that I have encountered starts from the individual herself and her attempt to know herself.[21] And because I hope to "reweave the spirit"—not only the spirit of my students and my readers, but also my own.

Much of the early impulse or motive for philosophy is autobiographical, as philosophy instructors are reminded each year when our first-year students arrive in our classes with questions about the meaning of life, that is, the meaning of their own lives. They want to understand themselves, their values, their beliefs, and their place within the universe. When philosophy is explicitly recognized to be, in part, an expression of personal history and social identity, we notice that part of the value of philosophizing is not only the insight gained into the chosen topic, but also insight gained into oneself[22]—construing "oneself" to mean not just one's own person, but oneself as a participant in various social communities and as a member of the human species.

What the feminist insistence on the relationships between philosophers and philosophical inquiry has

---

21 As my frequent references indicate, the work of Marilyn Frye (1983, 1992) is my favourite example.

22 Thus Joyce Trebilcot, for example, says that what most interests her as a philosopher is "how a particular issue [is] connected with who I am and who I want to be—a matter of why *I* should be working on *this* topic" (Trebilcot 1991, 45, her emphasis).

accomplished is to remind scholars that philosophy is deeply rooted in our personal histories and social identities. For the most part, philosophy is not, or is not only, an impersonal,[23] merely "academic" (in its several senses) or theoretical "discipline," something with which we engage only during business hours. It is also a living practice of self-knowledge. Philosophy is autobiographical. At its very best, it enables us not only to know ourselves, but also thereby to recreate ourselves. In understanding who we are, we are empowered to re-evaluate our vision, our projects, our sense of the purpose and the unfolding of our lives within the context of other lives.

Of course, feminist philosophical inquiry is not subsumed by self; philosophy is not just about individual philosophers, or even philosophers considered as the producers of a collective subject. Philosophical inquiry is not by any means only about personal history and social identity. As Jacqueline Jones points out:

> Obviously, all of us are composed of multiple, overlapping spheres of identity.... Obviously, the whole notion of matching any single personal demographic characteristic to one's teaching and scholarship is absurd on the face of it. (Jones 1996, 180-181)

Moreover, I am not denying the value of non-experiential writing or of work that is entirely theoretical. To teach and write from personal experience does not mean

---

23 As Williams puts it, "What is 'impersonal' writing but denial of self?" (Williams 1991, 92).

producing work that is pre-theoretical or untheorized, or that is raw, unsophisticated, or unthoughtful. My own courses and publications are not *about* my experience, nor are they limited to it. I do not require or compel my students to use their own experience. I am fully committed, under appropriate academic circumstances, to teaching and writing about impersonal and theoretical matters, and to teaching and writing about "what I am not" and what I have not experienced. While I am trying to explain and justify my own use of personal histories and social identities within philosophical inquiry, I am not thereby saying that this is the only defensible way to do philosophy, or that all other approaches to philosophical thought are somehow either mistaken or self-deluded, or even that the dangers of using arguments from personal experiences are always outweighed by the dangers of not using them (Ford 1997, 3).

What I am saying is that non-feminist philosophers may have something to learn from feminist philosophers' consciousness—indeed, self-consciousness—of the context and situatedness of philosophical inquiry. Such a self-consciousness may foster a deeper awareness both of the presuppositions and of the potential limits of one's philosophical work, and thereby promote greater philosophical objectivity, in the sense of absence of unrecognized and inappropriate biases. Failure to be aware of one's personal history and social identity in philosophical inquiry could cause one uncritically to take one's personal situation as universally applicable, or to fail to notice those aspects of one's identity that compromise one's understanding of, for example, a moral issue. At the same time, since philosophy begins with the self, begins with autobiography, begins with personal history and social identity, it remains a possible source of self-under-standing and self-knowledge like no other.

Moreover, within both writing and teaching, the problems that are generated by the use of personal history and social identity always become, or are capable of becoming, the focus of philosophical investigation, so that the appeal to experience is not a substitute but rather an occasion for the development of philosophical theory. In my classes I insist that while personal attacks are utterly unjustified, it is both possible and desirable to assess the ideas that originate from personal experiences. The fact that experience is mediated and is partly an ide-ological product is something philosophy students can learn and feminist scholars can recognize, and it provides all the more reason for investigating experience, as Diana Fuss proposes:

> [E]mpirical facts are always ideological productions ... [I]n terms of pedagogical [and scholarly] theory, such a position permits the introduction of narratives of lived experience in to the classroom [and research] while at the same time challenging us to examine collectively the central role social and historical practices play in shaping and producing these narratives. (Fuss 1989, 118)

In addition, I remain convinced that the epistemic need for the explicit use of autobiography is part of what morally justifies its use in philosophical inquiry. "Private life as exhibitionism and performance is not the same thing as a politicized strategic use of private information that seeks to subvert the politics of domination" (hooks with McKinnon 1996, 823). But in relying on personal histories and social identities in teaching and research I am not fabricating essentialist claims about the nature of the self or about what it means to be a woman or to experience the world as a woman. I know that identities are constituted largely through social classifications and behaviours, and that there is no set of physical, psychological, or social characteristics that all women share.

Nor am I making an unsubtle claim of insight or special epistemic privilege, on behalf of myself or other minority group members. I do not claim to have access to arcane philosophical topics or knowledge that is literally not available to, for example, men (Lauritzen 1997, 95). In fact, unlike non-feminist philosophers, who sometimes argue as if they are discovering truths that apply to and can be applied by all human beings regardless of personal and social context, feminist philosophers are more likely to recognize the limitations of their experience, its situatedness, and its partial and individual character.[24] As hooks acknowledges, "[E]xperience [alone] does not make one an expert" (hooks 1994, 43). I am not making a virtue out of necessity; but I am saying that social necessity or inevitability—the conspicuousness of the

---

24 And even feminists, especially white, middle-class, heterosexual feminists, are not always successful in achieving modesty about the import of their experience. Because some of them have been guilty of universalizing the implications of their experience in ways that are not appropriate, they have been criticized by feminists of colour, working class feminists, and lesbian and bisexual feminists, for unjustified uses of the words "we" and "us."

minority group member—often produces epistemic virtue.[25]

In academic contexts where the detached and the impersonal are often valued as characteristics of good and serious academic work, the acknowledgement of and explicit attention to personal history and social identity within philosophical inquiry can be politically and intellectually honest and empowering. When used with respect for the dangers they may pose, personal histories and social identities can be avenues toward integrity in philosophical inquiry.[26]

In her discussion of the employment of autobiography in academic writing, Bernstein advocates the use of what she calls "reflexive confession," which is "primarily a questioning mode, one that imposes self-vigilance on the process of subject positioning both in language and

25 Hooks suggests, "Usually it is in a context where the experiential knowledge of students is being denied or negated that they may feel most determined to impress upon listeners both its value and its superiority to other ways of knowing" (hooks 1994, 88; cf. 84). Hence, the affirmation of the relevance and importance of our experiences diminishes students' (and maybe sometimes instructors') felt need to claim that experience alone gives them privileged insight.

26 I have been asked what features of a philosopher's personal history and social identities are relevant to her teaching and scholarly work, and what determines their relevance (Switzer 1997, 2). No *a priori* answers can be given; we must look and see. I have also been asked to what areas of philosophy personal history and social identity are relevant. Michelle Switzer proposes that they are particularly relevant to social and political philosophy, ethics, aesthetics, and philosophy of law (Switzer 1997, 4). Yet the work of feminist philosophers such as Maria Lugones (1996) and Caroline Whitbeck (1983) strongly suggests that personal histories and social identities may also be relevant to metaphysics and epistemology.

discourse and at a specific historical moment or a particular cultural space. Not a unilateral critique of power, reflexive confession instead registers its complicity with the institutions that structure its representation" (Bernstein 1992, 140).

It is my intention and hope that this book has exemplified, to some modest degree, the self-aware, self-critical, and politically sensitized use of personal histories and social identities within feminist philosophy.

References

Abella, Rosalie Silberman. 1991. The New Isms and Universities. *University Affairs* (August/September): 17.

Alcoff, Linda. 1988. Cultural Feminism Versus Post-Structuralism: The Identity Crisis in Feminist Theory. *Signs: Journal of Women in Culture and Society* 13 (3) (Spring): 405-36.

Allen, Paula Gunn, Lisa Alther, Rosellen Brown, Marge Piercy, Jayne Cortez, Ursula K. Le Guin, Audre Lorde, Jan Clausen, Joanna Russ, Jane Rule, and Hisaye Yamamoto. 1989. What I Do When I Write. *The Women's Review of Books* 6 (10-11): 23-29.

American Philosophical Association Committee on the Status of Women. 1995. The Status of Senior Women in Philosophy. *American Philosophical Association Proceedings.* (May)

Anderson, Melissa A., Karen Seashore Louis, and Jason Earle. 1994. Disciplinary and Departmental Effects on Observations of Faculty and Graduate Student Misconduct. *The Journal of Higher Education.* 65 (3) (May/June): 331-50.

Ardis, Ann. 1992. Presence of Mind, Presence of Body: Embodying Positionality in the Classroom. *Hypatia: A Journal of Feminist Philosophy* 7 (2) (Spring): 167-76.

Backstrom, Kirsten. 1990. Rogue. *Trivia: A Journal of Ideas* 16/17: 11-17.

Bar On, Bat-Ami. 1993. Marginality and Epistemic Privilege. *Feminist Epistemologies.* Edited by Linda Alcoff and Elizabeth Porter. New York: Routledge. 83-100.

Bartky, Sandra Lee. 1988. Foucault, Femininity, and the Modernization of Patriarchal Power. *Feminism and Foucault: Reflections on Resistance.* Edited by Irene Diamond and Lee Quinby. Boston: Northeastern University Press. 61-86.

———. 1990. *Femininity and Domination: Studies in the Phenomenology of Oppression.* New York: Routledge.

Bernstein, Richard. 1990. 'Politically Correct' Attitudes at University. *The Kingston Whig-Standard* 30 October: 1-2.

Bernstein, Susan David. 1992. Confessing Feminist Theory: What's 'I' Got to Do With It? *Hypatia: A Journal of Feminist Philosophy* 7 (2) (Spring): 120-47.

Bickenbach, Jerome E. 1993. *Physical Disability and Social Policy.* Toronto, Ontario: University of Toronto Press.

Bordo, Susan. 1988. Feminist Skepticism and the 'Maleness' of Philosophy. *The Journal of Philosophy* 85 (11): 619-29.

———. 1990. Feminism, Postmodernism, and Gender-Scepticism. *Feminism/Postmodernism.* Edited by Linda J. Nicholson. New York: Routledge. 133-56.

Brison, Susan. 1997. Outliving Oneself: Trauma, Memory, and Personal Identity. *Feminists Rethink the Self.* Edited by Diana Tietjens Meyers. Boulder, Colorado: Westview Press. 12-39.

Brittan, Arthur. 1989. *Masculinity and Power.* Oxford: Basil Blackwell.

BrotherPeace. 1990. Poster. Ottawa, Ontario.

Butler, Judith. 1990. *Gender Trouble: Feminism and the Subversion of Identity.* New York: Routledge.

Cahn, Steven M. 1986. *Saints and Scamps: Ethics in Academia.* Totowa, New Jersey: Rowman & Littlefield.

Cardea, Caryatis. 1991-92. All the Pieces I Never Wrote About Class. *Sinister Wisdom* 45 (Winter): 105-17.

Carpenter, Mary Wilson. 1996. Female Grotesques in Academia: Ageism, Antifeminism, and Feminists on the Faculty. *Antifeminism in the Academy*. Edited by VéVé Clark, Shirley Nelson Garner, Margaret Higonnet, and Ketu H. Katrak. New York: Routledge. 141-65.

Childers, Mary, and bell hooks. 1990. A Conversation about Race and Class. *Conflicts in Feminism*. Edited by Marianne Hirsch and Evelyn Fox Keller. New York: Routledge. 60-81.

Coffin, Tammis. 1992. The Situation for 'People Raised Working-Class Now Working at Middle-Class Jobs.' *Present Time* 24 (2): 45-48.

Cohen, G.A. 1986. The Structure of Proletarian Unfreedom. *Analytical Marxism*. Edited by John Roemer. Cambridge: Cambridge University Press. 237-59.

Clark, Christopher M. 1986. Teachers as Designers in Self-Directed Professional Development. *Understanding Teacher Development*. Edited by A. Hargreaves and M. Fullan. New York: Teachers College Press. 75-84.

Clark, Lorenne M.G., and Lynda Lange, eds. 1979. *The Sexism of Social and Political Theory: Women and Reproduction From Plato to Nietzsche*. Toronto: University of Toronto Press.

Code, Lorraine, Sheila Mullett, and Christine Overall, eds. 1988. *Feminist Perspectives: Philosophical Essays On Method and Morals*. Toronto: University of Toronto Press.

Collins, Michael J., ed. 1983. *Teaching Values and Ethics in College*. San Francisco: Jossey-Bass.

Collins, Patricia Hill. 1996. The Social Construction of Black Feminist Thought. *Women, Knowledge, and Reality: Explorations in Feminist Philosophy*. 2nd ed. Edited by Ann Garry and Marilyn Pearsall. New York: Routledge. 222-48.

Copper, Baba. 1988. *Over the Hill: Reflections on Ageism Between Women*. Freedom, California: Crossing Press.

Courtot, Martha. 1991-92. Confessions of a Working-Class Intellectual. *Sinister Wisdom* 45 (Winter): 88-92.

Crane, David. 1995. A Personal Postscript. *Pedagogy: The Question of Impersonation*. Edited by Jane Gallop. Bloomington: Indiana University Press. ix-xiv.

Crow, Liz. 1996. Including All of Our Lives: Renewing the Social Model of Disability. *Encounters With Strangers: Feminism and Disability*. Edited by Jenny Morris. London: Women's Press. 206-26.

Davis, Barbara Hillyer. Teaching the Feminist Minority. *Gendered Subjects: The Dynamics of Feminist Teaching*. Edited by Margo Culley and Catherine Portuges. Boston: Routledge & Kegan Paul. 245-52.

Davis, Lennard J. 1995. *Enforcing Normalcy: Disability, Deafness and the Body*. London: Verso.

Delmar, Rosalind. 1986. What is Feminism? *What is Feminism?* Edited by Juliet Mitchell and Ann Oakley. Oxford: Basil Blackwell. 8-33.

Descartes, René. [1642] 1985. *Meditations on First Philosophy*. Translated with an introduction by Laurence J. Lafleur. New York: Macmillan.

duCille, Ann. 1994. The Occult of True Black Womanhood: Critical Demeanor and Black Feminist Studies. *Signs: Journal of Women in Culture and Society* 19 (3) (Spring): 591-629.

Elliott. 1991-92. Funeral Food. *Sinister Wisdom* 45 (Winter): 34-39.

Ellis, Carolyn. 1995. *Final Negotiations: A Story of Love, Loss, and Chronic Illness*. Philadelphia: Temple University Press.

Fennell, Tom. 1991. The Silencers. *Maclean's* 104 (21): 40-43.

Ferguson, Kathy E. 1991. Interpretation and Genealogy in Feminism. *Signs: Journal of Women in Culture and Society* 16 (2): 322-39.

Ford, Maureen. 1997. Legitimate Personal Experience and Ethico-Political Assessments of the Main Danger. Unpublished commentary on Personal Experience, Social Identities, and Feminist Inquiry. Presented at Annual Conference of the Canadian Society for Women in Philosophy, Dalhousie University, 28 September.

Frey, Olivia. 1993. Beyond Literary Darwinism: Women's Voices and Critical Discourse. *The Intimate Critique: Autobiographical Literary Criticism*. Edited by Diane P. Freedman, Olivia Frey, and Frances Murphy Zauhar. Durham: Duke University Press. 41-65.

Friedman, Amy. 1990. Politically Incorrect. *Kingston Whig-Standard Magazine* 24 November: 26-27.

Friedman, Susan Stanford. 1985. Authority in the Feminist Classroom: A Contradiction in Terms? *Gendered Subjects: The Dynamics of Feminist Teaching*. Edited by Margo Culley and Catherine Portuges. Boston: Routledge & Kegan Paul. 203-08.

Frost, Linda. 1997. 'Somewhere in Particular': Generations, Feminism, Class Conflict, and the Terms of Academic Success. *Generations: Academic Feminists In Dialogue*. Edited by Devoney Looser and E. Ann Kaplan. Minneapolis: University of Minnesota Press. 219-36.

Frye, Marilyn. 1983. *The Politics of Reality: Essays in Feminist Theory*. Freedom, California: Crossing Press.

———. 1992. *Willful Virgin: Essays in Feminism 1976-1992*. Freedom, California: Crossing Press.

Fuss, Diana. 1989. *Essentially Speaking: Feminism, Nature and Difference*. New York: Routledge.

Gallop, Jane. 1995. Im-Personation. *Pedagogy: The Question of Impersonation*. Edited by Jane Gallop. Bloomington: Indiana University Press. 1-18.

Garry, Ann, and Marilyn Pearsall, eds. 1989. *Women, Knowledge, and Reality: Explorations in Feminist Philosophy*. Boston: Unwin Hyman.

Garvin, David A. 1991. A Delicate Balance: Ethical Dilemmas and the Discussion Process. *Education for Judgment: The Artistry of Discussion Leadership.* Edited by C. Roland Christensen, David A. Garvin, and Ann Sweet. Boston: Harvard Business School Press. 287-303.

Garvin, Joyce. 1991. Undue Influence: Confessions From an Uneasy Discussion Leader. *Education for Judgment: The Artistry of Discussion Leadership.* Edited by C. Roland Christensen, David A. Garvin, and Ann Sweet. Boston: Harvard Business School Press. 275-86.

Greene, Gayle, and Coppélia Kahn, eds. 1993. *Changing Subjects: The Making of Feminist Literary Criticism.* New York: Routledge.

Griffiths, Morwenna, and Margaret Whitford, eds. 1988. *Feminist Perspectives In Philosophy.* Bloomington: Indiana University Press.

Grimshaw, Jean. 1986. *Philosophy and Feminist Thinking.* Minneapolis: University of Minnesota Press.

Grumet, Madeleine R. 1995. *Scholae Personae:* Masks for Meaning. *Pedagogy: The Question of Impersonation.* Edited by Jane Gallop. Bloomington: Indiana University Press. 36-45.

Harding, Sandra. 1986. *The Science Question in Feminism.* Ithaca: Cornell University Press.

———. 1990. Feminism, Science, and the Anti-Enlightenment Critiques. *Feminism/Postmodernism.* Edited by Linda J. Nicholson. New York: Routledge. 83-106.

———. 1993. Rethinking Standpoint Epistemology: 'What is Strong Objectivity?' *Feminist Epistemologies.* Edited by Linda Alcoff and Elizabeth Porter. New York: Routledge. 49-82.

Harding, Sandra, and Merrill B. Hintikka, eds. 1983. *Discovering Reality: Feminist Perspectives On Epistemology, Metaphysics, Methodology, and Philosophy of Science.* Dordrecht: D. Reidel.

Hartsock, Nancy C. M. 1986. The Feminist Standpoint: Developing the Ground for a Specifically Feminist Historical Materialism. *Discovering Reality: Feminist Perspectives On Epistemology, Metaphysics, Methodology, and Philosophy of Science.* Edited by Sandra Harding and Merrill B. Hintikka. Dordrecht: D. Reidel. 283-310.

Heath, Stephen. 1987a. Male Feminism. *Men in Feminism.* Edited by Alice Jardine and Paul Smith. New York: Methuen. 1-32.

———. 1987b. Men in Feminism: Men and Feminist Theory. *Men in Feminism.* Edited by Alice Jardine and Paul Smith. New York: Methuen. 41-46.

Heilbrun, Carolyn G. 1998. Women's Written Lives: The View from the Threshold. CBC Radio "Ideas," 28, 29 January.

Hildebidle, John. 1991. Having It by Heart: Some Reflections on Knowing Too Much. *Education for Judgment: The Artistry of Discussion Leadership.* Edited by C. Roland Christensen, David A. Garvin, and Ann Sweet. Boston: Harvard Business School Press. 265-74.

Hillyer, Barbara. 1993. *Feminism and Disability.* Norman, Oklahoma: University of Oklahoma Press.

hooks, bell. 1988. *Talking Back: Thinking Feminist, Thinking Black.* Toronto: Between the Lines.

———. 1994. *Teaching to Transgress: Education as the Practice of Freedom.* New York: Routledge.

hooks, bell, with Tanya McKinnon. 1996. Sisterhood: Beyond Public and Private. *Signs: Journal of Women in Culture and Society* 21 (4) (Summer): 814-29.

Isaacs-Doyle, Jane. 1998. Unpublished commentary on Personal Histories, Social Identities, and Feminist Philosophical Inquiry. Presented at Queen's University Department of Philosophy Colloquium Series, 5 February.

Jackins, Harvey. 1973. *The Human Situation.* Seattle: Rational Island Publishers.

————. 1978a. *The Human Side of Human Beings: The Theory of Re-evaluation Counseling*. Seattle: Rational Island Publishers.

————. 1978b. *The Upward Trend*. Seattle: Rational Island Publishers.

————. 1981. *The Benign Reality*. Seattle: Rational Island Publishers.

————. 1983. *The Reclaiming of Power*. Seattle: Rational Island Publishers.

————. 1985. *The Rest of Our Lives*. Seattle: Rational Island Publishers.

————. 1987. *The Longer View*. Seattle: Rational Island Publishers.

————. 1989. *Start Over Every Morning*. Seattle: Rational Island Publishers.

————. 1992. *A Better World*. Seattle: Rational Island Publishers.

Jaggar, Alison. 1989. Love and Knowledge: Emotion in Feminist Epistemology. *Women, Knowledge, and Reality: Explorations In Feminist Philosophy*. Edited by Ann Garry and Marilyn Pearsall. Boston: Unwin Hyman. 129-55.

Jones, Craig. 1990. The Rationale of Gender Terror—Why Women Fear Men. *The Queen's Journal* (30 March): 15.

Jones, Jacqueline. 1996. Teaching What the Truth Compels You to Teach: A Historian's View. *Teaching What You're Not: Identity Politics in Higher Education*. Edited by Katherine J. Mayberry. New York: New York University Press. 177-94.

Karamcheti, Indira. 1995. Caliban in the Classroom. *Pedagogy: The Question of Impersonation*. Edited by Jane Gallop. Bloomington: Indiana University Press. 138-46.

Kaplan, Alice. 1993. *French Lessons: A Memoir*. Chicago: University of Chicago Press.

————. 1997. The Trouble With Memoir. *The Chronicle of Higher Education* 44 (15) (5 December): B4-B5.

Keith, Lois. 1996. Encounters With Strangers: The Public's Responses to Disabled Women and How This Affects Our Sense of Self. *Encounters With Strangers: Feminism and Disability.* Edited by Jenny Morris. London: Women's Press. 69-88.

Keller, Evelyn Fox and Helen Moglen. 1987. Competition: A Problem for Academic Women. *Competition: A Feminist Taboo?* Edited by Valerie Miner and Helen E. Longino. New York: Feminist Press. 21-37.

Kuhn, Annette. 1995. *Family Secrets: Acts of Memory and Imagination.* London: Verso.

Lauritzen, Paul. 1997. Hear No Evil, See No Evil, Think No Evil: Ethics and the Appeal to Experience. *Hypatia: A Journal of Feminist Philosophy* 12 (2) (Spring): 83-104.

Le Doeuff, Michele. 1990. *Hipparchia's Choice: An Essay Concerning Women, Philosophy, Etc.*. Oxford: Basil Blackwell.

Levy, Allen. 1986. Allies of Parents and Young People Workshop." *The Re-Evaluation Counseling Teacher* 21: 48.

Litvak, Joseph. 1995. Discipline, Spectacle, and Melancholia in and around the Gay Studies Classroom. *Pedagogy: The Question of Impersonation.* Edited by Jane Gallop. Bloomington: Indiana University Press. 19-27.

Livia, Anna. 1989. You Can Only Be Wrong... *The Women's Review of Books* 6 (10-11): 33-34.

Lloyd, Genevieve. 1984. *The Man of Reason: "Male" and "Female" in Western Philosophy.* Minneapolis: University of Minnesota Press.

Longino, Helen. 1993. Subjects, Power and Knowledge: Description and Prescription in Feminist Philosophies of Science. *Feminist Epistemologies.* Edited by Linda Alcoff and Elizabeth Porter. New York: Routledge. 101-20.

Lugones, Maria [C.]. 1989. Playfulness, "World"-Traveling, and Loving Perception. *Women, Knowledge, and Reality: Explorations in Feminist Philosophy.* Edited by Ann Garry and Marilyn Pearsall. Boston: Unwin Hyman. 275-90.

Lugones, Maria C. and Elizabeth V. Spelman. 1987. Competition, Compassion, and Community: Models for a Feminist Ethos. *Competition: A Feminist Taboo?*. Edited by Valerie Miner and Helen E. Longino. New York: Feminist Press. 234-47.

MacGregor, Sharilyn. 1990. Notions of 'Political Correctness' Discouraging. *The Queen's Journal* 16 October: 10.

Mairs, Nancy. 1990. *Carnal Acts: Essays*. New York: HarperCollins.

———— 1996. *Waist-High in the World: A Life Among the Nondisabled*. Boston: Beacon Press.

Martin, Jane Roland. 1994. Methodological Essentialism, False Difference, and Other Dangerous Traps. *Signs: Journal of Women In Culture and Society* 19 (3) (Spring): 630-57.

Mayberry, Katherine J. 1996. Ed. *Teaching What You're Not: Identity Politics in Higher Education*. New York: New York University Press.

McAlister, Linda Lopez, and Joanne Waugh. 1997. Preface. *Hypatia: A Journal of Feminist Philosophy* 12 (1): vii-ix.

McCarthy, Mary. 1951. *The Groves of Academe*. New York: Harcourt, Brace & World.

Medical Research Council. 1994. *Vignettes in Scientific Integrity*. Ottawa: Medical Research Council.

Middleton, Sue. 1993. *Educating Feminists: Life Histories and Pedagogy*. New York: Teachers College Press.

Miles, Angela. 1991. Confessions of a Harlequin Reader: Romance and the Myth of Male Mothers. *The Hysterical Male: New Feminist Theory*. Edited by Arthur Kroker and Marilouise Kroker. Montreal: New World Perspectives. 93-131.

Miller, Nancy K. 1991. *Getting Personal: Feminist Occasions and Other Autobiographical Acts*. New York: Routledge.

————. 1997. Public Statements, Private Lives: Academic Memoirs for the Nineties. *Signs: Journal of Women in Culture and Society* 22 (4) (Summer): 981-1015.

Miller, Susan. 1995. *In Loco Parentis*: Addressing (the) Class. *Pedagogy: The Question of Impersonation*. Edited by Jane Gallop. Bloomington: Indiana University Press. 155-64.

Morgan, Kathryn Pauly. 1987. The Perils and Paradoxes of Feminist Pedagogy. *Resources for Feminist Research/Documentation sur la recherche féministe* 16 (3): 49-52.

Morris, Jenny. 1991. *Pride Against Prejudice: Transforming Attitudes to Disability*. London: Women's Press.

Moulton, Janice. 1989. A Paradigm of Philosophy: The Adversary Method. *Women, Knowledge, and Reality: Explorations in Feminist Philosophy*. Edited by Ann Garry and Marilyn Pearsall. Boston: Unwin Hyman. 5-20.

Murphy, Marilyn. 1991. Did Your Mother Do Volunteer Work? An Introduction to the Class Issue. *Lesbian Ethics* 4 (2): 28-40.

Nelson, Mariah Burton. 1991. The Rules of the Game. *Women's Review of Books* 8 (4) (January): 17.

Nickerson, Dan. 1991. Being Sensible About Class Divisions. *Present Time* 22 (1) (January): 53-58.

Nozick, Robert. 1981. *Philosophical Explanations*. Cambridge, Massachusetts: Belknap Press.

Offen, Karen. 1988. Defining Feminism: A Comparative Historical Approach. *Signs: Journal of Women in Culture and Society* 14 (1): 119-57.

O'Reilly, Mary Rose. 1993. *The Peaceable Classroom*. Portsmouth, New Hampshire: Boynton-Cook.

Overall, Christine. 1987a. *Ethics and Human Reproduction: A Feminist Analysis*. Boston: Allen & Unwin.

————. 1987b. Role Models: A Critique. *Women: Isolation and Bonding—The Ecology of Gender*. Edited by Kathleen Storrie. Toronto: Methuen. 179-86.

————. 1988. Feminism, Ontology, and "Other Minds." *Feminist Perspectives: Philosophical Essays on Method and Morals*. Edited by Lorraine Code, Sheila Mullett, and Christine Overall. Toronto: University of Toronto Press. 89-106.

————. 1993. *Human Reproduction: Principles, Practices, Policies*. Toronto: Oxford University Press.

————. 1995. "Nowhere at Home": Toward a Phenomenology of Working Class Consciousness. *This Fine Place So Far From Home: Voices of Academics from the Working Class*. Edited by C. L. Barney Dews and Carolyn Leste Law. Philadelphia: Temple University Press. 209-20.

————. 1996. Reflections of a Sceptical Bioethicist. *Philosophical Perspectives on Bioethics*. Edited by Joseph Boyle and L.W. Sumner. Toronto: University of Toronto Press. 163-86.

Ozar, David T. 1993. Building Awareness of Ethical Standards and Conduct. *Educating Professionals: Responding to New Expectations for Competence and Accountability*. Edited by Lynn Curry, Jon F. Wergin and Associates. San Francisco: Jossey-Bass. 148-77.

Page, Joanne. 1990. Untitled unpublished essay.

Perillo, Lucia. 1997. When the Classroom Becomes a Confessional. *The Chronicle of Higher Education* 44 (14) (28 November).

Prado, Carlos. 1998. Not So Free Speech. *The Hamilton Examiner* no. 4 (May).

Ruddick, Sara. 1983. Maternal Thinking. *Mothering: Essays in Feminist Theory*. Edited by Joyce Trebilcot. Totowa, New Jersey: Rowman & Allanheld. 213-30.

————. 1995. *Maternal Thinking: Toward a Politics of Peace*. Boston: Beacon Press.

Quinby, Lee. 1992. The Subject of Memoirs: *The Woman Warrior*'s Technology of Ideographic Selfhood. *De/Colonizing the Subject: The Politics of Gender in Women's Autobiography.* Edited by Sidonie Smith and Julia Watson. Minneapolis: University of Minnesota Press. 297-320.

Rich, Adrienne. 1985. Taking Women Students Seriously. *Gendered Subjects: The Dynamics of Feminist Teaching.* Edited by Margo Culley and Catherine Portuges. Boston: Routledge & Kegan Paul. 21-28.

Ross, Paula. 1987. Women, Oppression, Privilege, and Competition. *Competition: A Feminist Taboo?* Edited by Valerie Miner and Helen E. Longino. New York: Feminist Press. 209-20.

Rubin, Gayle. 1975. The Traffic in Women: Notes on the "Political Economy" of Sex. *Toward an Anthropology of Women.* Edited by Rayna R. Rapp. New York: Monthly Review Press. 157-210.

Ruth, Sheila. 1981. Methodocracy, Misogyny, and Bad Faith: The Response of Philosophy. *Men's Studies Modified: The Impact of Feminism on the Academic Disciplines.* Oxford: Pergamon Press. 43-53.

Ryan, Jake, and Charles Sackrey. 1984. *Strangers in Paradise: Academics From the Working Class.* Boston: South End Press.

Sartwell, Crispin. 1998. Addiction and Authorship. Presented at the Annual Meeting of the Canadian Philosophical Association, Congress of the Social Sciences and Humanities, University of Ottawa, 29 May.

Scheman, Naomi. 1995. On Waking Up One Morning and Discovering We are Them. *Pedagogy: The Question of Impersonation.* Edited by Jane Gallop. Bloomington: Indiana University Press. 106-16.

Scholes, Robert. 1987. Reading Like a Man. *Men in Feminism.* Edited by Alice Jardine and Paul Smith. New York: Methuen. 204-18.

Segal, Lynne. 1990. *Slow Motion: Changing Masculinities, Changing Men.* London: Virago.

Shalit, Ruth. 1998. The Man Who Knew Too Much. *Lingua Franca* 8 (1) (February): 31-40.

Sherwin, Susan. 1988. Philosophical Methodology and Feminist Methodology: Are They Compatible? *Feminist Perspectives: Philosophical Essays on Method and Morals.* Edited by Lorraine Code, Sheila Mullett, and Christine Overall. Toronto: University of Toronto Press. 13-28.

Smith, Sidonie, and Julia Watson. 1992. Introduction. *De/Colonizing the Subject: The Politics of Gender in Women's Autobiography.* Edited by Sidonie Smith and Julia Watson. Minneapolis: University of Minnesota Press. xiii-xxxi.

———. 1996. Introduction. *Getting a Life: Everyday Uses of Autobiography.* Edited by Sidonie Smith and Julia Watson. Minneapolis: University of Minnesota Press. 1-24.

Snitow, Ann. 1990. A Gender Diary. *Conflicts in Feminism.* Edited by Marianne Hirsch and Evelyn Fox Keller. New York: Routledge. 1-43.

Spender, Dale. 1985. *Man Made Language.* 2d ed. London: Routledge and Kegan Paul.

Steedman, Carolyn Kay. 1987. *Landscape for a Good Woman: A Story of Two Lives.* New Brunswick, New Jersey: Rutgers.

Stoltenberg, John. 1990. *Refusing to Be a Man: Essays on Sex and Justice.* New York: Penguin Books.

Story, Medicine. 1989. Sons of Earth and Sky. *Men* (4) 47-54.

Svinicki, Marilla. 1994. Ethics in College Teaching. *Teaching Tips: Strategies, Research, and Theory for College and University Teachers.* 9th ed. Edited by Wilbert J. McKeachie. Lexington, Massachusetts: D.C. Heath. 269-77.

Switzer, Michelle. 1997. Unpublished commentary on Personal History, Social Identity, and Philosophical Inquiry. Presented at Looking Back, Looking Forward: Philosophy, Its History and Future, a Conference to Celebrate the Centenary of the Philosophy Doctoral Program, Department of Philosophy, University of Toronto, 24 October.

Talbot, Margaret. 1994. A Most Dangerous Method. *Lingua Franca* 4 (2) (January/February): 24-40.

Tancred-Sheriff, Peta. 1990. On Reviewing and Being Reviewed. *Institut Simone de Beauvoir Institute Bulletin/Newsletter* 10 (1): 31-33.

Thielen-Wilson, Leslie. 1988. Befriending Bearded-Mothers. Presented at the Panel Discussion on Power and Competition: Their Effects on Relations Among Academic Feminists. Annual Meeting of the Canadian Society for Women in Philosophy, Edmonton, Alberta.

Tokarczyk, Michelle M., and Elizabeth A. Fay. 1993. *Working Class Women in the Academy: Laborers in the Knowledge Factory.* Amherst: University of Massachusetts Press.

Tompkins, Jane. 1989. Me and My Shadow. *Gender and Theory: Dialogues on Feminist Criticism.* Edited by Linda Kauffman. Oxford: Basil Blackwell. 121-39.

———. 1991. Teaching Like it Matters: A Modest Proposal for Revolutionizing the Classroom. *Lingua Franca* 1 (6) (August, 1991): 24-27.

Torgovnick, Marianna De Marco. 1994. *Crossing Ocean Parkway: Readings by an Italian American Daughter.* Chicago: University of Chicago Press.

Trebilcot, Joyce. 1991. Ethics of Method: Greasing the Machine and Telling Stories. *Feminist Ethics.* Edited by Claudia Card. Lawrence: University Press of Kansas. 45-51.

———. 1994. *Dyke Ideas: Process, Politics, Daily Life.* Albany, New York: State University of New York.

Tremain, Shelley. 1996. We're Here. We're Disabled and Queer. Get Used to It. *Pushing the Limits: Disabled Dykes Produce Culture*. Edited by Shelley Tremain. Toronto: Toronto Women's Press. 15-24.

Wendell, Susan. 1989. Toward a Feminist Theory of Disability. *Hypatia: A Journal of Feminist Philosophy* 4 (2): 104-24.

———. 1996. *The Rejected Body: Feminist Philosophical Reflections on Disability*. New York: Routledge.

Whitbeck, Caroline. 1983. A Different Reality: Feminist Ontology. *Beyond Domination: New Perspectives on Women and Philosophy*. Edited by Carol C. Gould. Totowa, New Jersey: Rowman & Allanheld. 64-88.

Williams, Patricia J. 1991. *The Alchemy of Race and Rights: Diary of a Law Professor*. Cambridge: Harvard University Press.

Winslow, Carie. 1991-1992. A Poor Girl Comes Clean. *Sinister Wisdom* 45 (Winter): 49-52.

Young-Bruehl, Elisabeth. 1991. Pride and Prejudice: Feminist Scholars Reclaim the First Person. *Lingua Franca* 1 (3) (February): 15-19; 33.